Ben Franklin's
ALMANAC

BEING A TRUE ACCOUNT OF THE GOOD GENTLEMAN'S LIFE

Candace Fleming

AN ANNE SCHWARTZ BOOK

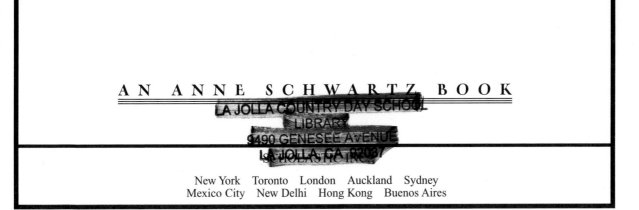

SCHOLASTIC INC.

New York   Toronto   London   Auckland   Sydney
Mexico City   New Delhi   Hong Kong   Buenos Aires

ACKNOWLEDGMENTS

This book could not have been written without the help of many people. I am indebted to Roy Goodman, Valerie-Anne Lutz, and Robert Cox of the American Philosophical Society for patiently searching through numerous sources to find the very one I needed; Ellen Cohn and Natalie Lesueur of the Benjamin Franklin Collection at Yale University for searching out facts, tracking down photographs, and sharing that vast Franklin material; Sue Levy at the Cigna Museum and Art Collection for generously allowing use of the museum's Franklin portraits; Holly Pribble and Eric Rohmann for contributing their considerable talents; Mrs. Jackson C. Boswell for graciously allowing her portrait of William Franklin to appear in these pages; and the superb and tireless staff at the Library of Congress who worked miracles obtaining obscure and out-of-print materials.

I would also like to thank Christopher Looby, professor of English at the University of California, Los Angeles, as well as Edward Martin, history teacher at the Berkeley Carroll School in Brooklyn, New York, for reading the manuscript with an eye for facts and a deep understanding of the subject.

And last, but not least, I am especially grateful to my editor, Anne Schwartz, whose advice and support have been constantly available—and invaluable.

ISBN 0-439-66956-1

12 11 10 9 8 7 6 5 4 3 2 1   4 5 6 7 8 9/0

Printed in the U.S.A.   08

First Scholastic printing, September 2004

Book design by Patti Ratchford

The text for this book is set in Oneleigh.

A NOTE ABOUT THE TEXT: Because history is not an exact discipline, dates sometimes vary among source materials. In most cases when discrepancies occurred, the author used Carl Van Doren's account of events. Most quotations have been excerpted from longer, original documents. Original spelling and punctuation have been modernized for readability and clarity.

CONTENTS

Courteous Reader:

Ben Franklin once said, "A man's story is not told solely by a list of his grand accomplishments, but rather by his smaller, daily goods." It is those "smaller goods" this book focuses on. Within its pages you will, of course, find mementos of his most famous achievements. After all, what book about Ben Franklin would be complete without mention of electricity, the American Revolution, or *Poor Richard's Almanack*? But you will also find scraps from some lesser-known events, as well as funny stories, hand-drawn sketches, cartoons of the day, and snippets of gossip. You will find souvenirs from Ben's travels, keepsakes from his childhood, bits of his family life, and pieces of his private thoughts.

What you won't find is a chronological order to these bits and pieces—this is not your traditional biography. Of course, when I began the project, I meant to write one. But as I read Ben's letters and essays, looked at pictures of his family, and uncovered Franklin stories and anecdotes, I began to see him differently. Innovative, vulgar, sometimes heroic, sometimes flawed, the incredibly complex Ben Franklin I discovered beguiled me, and I was no longer satisfied to tell his story in the ordinary way. I needed a form that would illuminate each of the many facets of his life—the vastness of his interests and accomplishments, and the deep commitment he made to each one.

Ultimately, I hit upon the idea of gathering the bits and pieces by subject and putting them in chapters with titles such as "Boyhood Memories," "The Writer's Journal," "Revolutionary Memorabilia," et cetera. By organizing the book in this way, I hope you will clearly see each of the many, varied interests Ben pursued throughout his long life. You will watch specific events as they unfold, particular ideas develop, and relationships progress. You will also be able to open this book to any page and discover a piece of Ben—as in a scrapbook. And by using the time line at the beginning, you can, if you wish, place this piece within the whole context of his life.

And like a scrapbook, the story of Ben's life has been centered around visuals—portraits, etchings, cartoons, and sketches. These images—most created long ago—will bring you face-to-face with history, and help you to connect with Ben the person, rather than just a name and dates. You will actually *see* Ben's childhood home. You will *see* his electrical equipment, the faces of his family, the first pages of his most famous writings. And hopefully, like the individual pieces of a jigsaw puzzle, these snapshots will come together and a whole picture of Ben Franklin will emerge.

Luckily for us, so much of his life has been preserved. It seems that Ben himself kept all his papers—every letter, pamphlet, rough draft, article, drawing, visiting card, invitation—everything! He cherished these papers, and with his strong sense of history, understood that one day they would be useful. When he died, he left them to his grandson William Temple Franklin.

Unfortunately, Temple did not cherish them. Dividing the collection, he left half the papers with a friend, who stored them in his barn. There they remained for the next thirty years, gathering dust, growing mildew, and being given away as gifts to various houseguests.

The other half of Ben's papers fared no better. Temple carried them to England, where he eventually abandoned them. Around 1840 they were discovered in a London tailor shop (Temple had once lived upstairs). Incredibly, the tailor had used them as patterns for the garments he was cutting.

All might have been lost if not for the efforts of institutions like the American Philosophical Society, Yale University, and the Library of Congress. Working independently of one another, these institutions rescued Ben's papers from barn and tailor shop. They searched out other mementos of Ben's life. They gathered, and are still gathering, many of the pieces together. They preserved them, published them, and cherished them as Ben would have. They also generously photographed them and made them available for the pages of this book.

Together these bits and pieces shape the story of Ben's life and show us his many sides—his intense commitment, his wise reasonableness, his sense of social justice, and his unfailing good humor. Indeed, they show us both his "grand accomplishments" and his "smaller goods."

Candace Fleming

A YEAR-BY-YEAR LOOK AT BEN'S LIFE

1706: Ben is born on Milk Street in Boston to Josiah and Abiah Franklin.

1712: Moves with his family to bigger house on Hanover Street

1714: Enters Boston Grammar (Latin) School

1715: Josiah decides he cannot afford the school and withdraws Ben. Enters Ben in Mr. Brownell's school.

1716: Josiah withdraws Ben from Mr. Brownell's school and puts him to work in his soap- and candlemaking shop.

1718: Josiah apprentices Ben to older brother James, a printer.

1721: James begins to publish his newspaper, the *New England Courant*.

1722: Massachusetts Assembly jails James for ridiculing public officials in his paper.

1723: Massachusetts Assembly forbids James to publish the *Courant*. James has Ben publish the paper for him, under Ben's name. Ben runs away to Philadelphia, gets a job as a printer, and finds a home with John Read, father of his future wife, Deborah.

1724: Governor William Keith sends Ben to London to buy equipment and materials for a printing shop he has promised to finance. Ben arrives to find none of Keith's promises kept. Finds work at Palmer's Printing House.

1726: Returns to Philadelphia and works in Thomas Denham's store until Denham dies. Ben returns to his former printing job.

1727: Forms the Junto, a philosophical/political discussion group

1728: Sets up own printing shop

1729: Publishes the first edition of the *Pennsylvania Gazette*

1730: Marries Deborah Read. Son William Franklin is born. Begins printing money for the colony of Pennsylvania.

1731: With the Junto, forms the Library Company of Philadelphia

1732: Son Francis Folger Franklin is born. Ben prints first edition of *Poor Richard's Almanack*.

1733: Embarks on self-improvement scheme

1736: Francis dies of smallpox. Ben establishes the Union Fire Company. Is appointed clerk of Pennsylvania Assembly. Begins promoting his city-wide sanitation scheme. Prints counterfeit-proof money for the colony of New Jersey.

1737: Becomes postmaster of Philadelphia

1741: Invents the Franklin stove. Publishes *The General Magazine.*

1743: Daughter Sally is born. Ben establishes framework for the formation of the American Philosophical Society.

1744: David Hall becomes Ben's partner in his printing business.

1745: Begins his electrical experiments

1748: Becomes a soldier in militia regiment he organizes. Retires from printing and turns business over to David Hall. Moves to a house away from noisy market center.

1749: Writes *Proposals Relating to the Education of Youth in Pennsylvania,* which convinces citizens that a state school is needed. This school eventually becomes the University of Pennsylvania.

1750: First suggests the use of lightning rods to keep houses safe

1751: Helps Dr. Thomas Bond establish the Pennsylvania Hospital. Ben's *Experiments and Observations on Electricity* is published in London.

1752: Performs famous kite experiment, proving lightning is electricity

1753: Receives honorary degrees from Harvard and Yale Universities. Is awarded the Copley Medal from the Royal Society of London. Is appointed deputy postmaster general for America and begins overhaul of the postal system. Helps negotiate a treaty with Native Americans. Mounts a lightning rod on his own roof.

1754: France and England begin fighting for control of North America. Appointed to the Albany Congress, Ben forms his Albany Plan of Union. Creates "Join, or Die" cartoon.

1756: French and Indian War declared. Oversees the construction of stockades on Pennsylvania's frontiers.

1757: Pennsylvania Assembly sends Ben to England to discuss colonial disputes with Parliament. During voyage, Ben writes "Father Abraham's Speech," the preface for the final edition of *Poor Richard's Almanack.*

1760: Grandson William Temple Franklin is born in London to unknown mother. Ben begins construction of his mansion in Philadelphia.

1761: Invents armonica

1762: Son, William, is appointed royal governor of New Jersey. Ben returns to Philadelphia.

1764: Condemns a group of Scottish Americans for attacking Native Americans. Returns to England to bring even more colonial disputes to Parliament's attention.

1765: Stamp Act is passed by Parliament. Angry Philadelphian mobs surround Ben's home.

1766: Testifies in favor of the repeal of the Stamp Act before the House of Commons. Testimony is published and applauded in America.

1767: Parliament passes the Townshend Acts, laying taxes on lead, paint, tea, and other items. Americans are outraged. Daughter Sally marries Richard Bache, a Philadelphian shopkeeper.

1768: The British send troops to Boston. Ben devises phonetic alphabet. Publishes first outline of the size and course of the Gulf Stream.

1769: Grandson Benjamin Franklin Bache is born in Philadelphia.

1770: The Boston Massacre occurs. Ben tries to bring compromise between England and the colonies.

1771: Begins writing his *Autobiography*

1773: Parliament passes the Tea Act, leading to the Boston Tea Party. Ben tries one last time for reconciliation between the two countries.

1774: Parliament passes the Intolerable Acts, punishing Boston for the Tea Party. Ben is ridiculed and denounced by Alexander Wedderburn, attorney for the king, before the Privy Council. He no longer sees any way for England and the colonies to reconcile. In Philadelphia, Deborah Franklin dies after suffering a stroke.

1775: The Battles of Lexington and Concord occur in April, marking the beginning of the Revolutionary War. Ben returns to Philadelphia and takes his seat in the First Continental Congress. Meets with General George Washington to determine the army's needs. Defeat of the Battle of Bunker Hill convinces Ben that independence is called for. Writes his own declaration.

1776: Is appointed by Congress to draft a declaration of independence. Thomas Jefferson writes it and asks Ben for input. Votes for independence on July 2. After Washington's defeat on Long Island, Ben is appointed commissioner to France. He sets sail with grandsons William Temple Franklin and Benjamin Franklin Bache. Arriving in Paris on

December 21, he hopes to convince the French government to form an alliance.

1777: Ben hears grim news of British occupation of Philadelphia. Also hears joyous news of American victory at Saratoga, New York. Meets Madame Helvétius.

1778: France formally recognizes the United States and signs Treaty of Alliance. Ben is appointed sole minister plenipotentiary by Congress. Begins writing the bagatelles.

1779: Ben and American naval officer John Paul Jones form a plan to raid the English coastline, resulting in a stunning naval victory for Jones.

1780: Gen. Charles Cornwallis takes control of British forces in the American colonies. French troops, under command of the Comte de Rochambeau, arrive in America.

1781: Cornwallis surrenders at Yorktown, putting an end to the Revolutionary War. Congress appoints Ben, along with John Jay, John Adams, and Henry Laurens, as commissioner to negotiate peace.

1782: Ben does not approve of Congress's choice of the bald eagle as an American symbol.

1783: Ben and the American commission complete negotiations and sign peace treaty with England. Ben attends first-ever launching of a hot-air balloon.

1784: Ben receives letter from son, William, now living in England. It is their first communication in twelve years. Invents bifocals. Exposes Friedrich Anton Mesmer as a fraud.

1785: Ben returns home. On way, meets son, William, in England. Is elected president of the executive council of Pennsylvania.

1786: Reelected president of Pennsylvania

1787: Serves third and final term as president of Pennsylvania. Also serves as the oldest delegate to the Constitutional Convention, where he proposes a two-house legislature. Becomes president of the Pennsylvania Society for Promoting the Abolition of Slavery.

1788: Retires from public office

1790: Sends letter and petition requesting slavery be outlawed to John Adams, vice president of the United States. Petition is denied, as Ben expected. Dies on April 17; buried next to Deborah in Christ Church Cemetery, Philadelphia.

BOYHOOD
MEMORIES

Imagining it may be . . . agreeable to you to learn the
circumstances of *my* life. . . . I sit down to write them.

—BENJAMIN FRANKLIN, *AUTOBIOGRAPHY, 1771*

Boston in the Early 1700s

A small town by modern standards, Boston was a bustling center of
Colonial America. Each person, big or small, had his share of work
to do. If a person didn't work, the government of the colony of
Massachusetts whipped or jailed him. Strict rules and harsh punishments were
enforced. Boston wasn't particularly pretty, either. Narrow, winding streets
full of bumps and holes climbed the low hills above the harbor. On either side
of the streets stood square, weathered-gray houses, about a thousand of them.
Geese honked on the Common, and pigs roamed the trash-strewn streets.
Still, Boston, with a population of nearly six thousand in 1706, was growing,
and its harbor had already become the busiest port in North America. As its
citizens knew, it would soon become a city to rival all others.

The city as it looked around the time of Ben's birth.

The cottage on Milk Street where Ben was born on January 17, 1706
On a bitterly cold morning Abiah Franklin gave birth to her eighth child (and father Josiah's fifteenth), a gray-eyed baby boy. Because it was Sunday and the congregation was in church anyway, Josiah bundled the infant into a quilt and carried him across the snow-covered street to Old South Church. There, with icy water from the baptismal font trickling down his forehead, the baby was christened Benjamin Franklin.

LIFE IN THE NEW WORLD

The first English settlers arrived in North America in the early 1600s. By the time Ben was born a hundred years later, thirteen English-speaking colonies hugged the Atlantic coast. Beyond them a great expanse of land rolled westward, nobody knew how far. This land was left to the Native Americans as white settlers learned to live in their new environment.

It was not an easy task. Land had to be cleared. Homes had to be built. Crops had to be planted. And all the while, settlers battled disease, malnutrition, Native American attacks, and the bitterly cold climate. Clean drinking water was often hard to find. Food was scarce. And one out of every four babies died before his or her first birthday.

Still people flocked from England to the New World. They came because life was freer in the colonies. America had its upper and lower classes, but it did not have barriers between them. With hard work, a man could climb to the top and become a prosperous, influential citizen.

He could also freely practice his religion. In America there were Quakers, Roman Catholics, Moravians, Jews, and Anabaptists. And although there had been religious strife early on (in the 1600s), by the time of Ben's birth, tolerance among the various religious groups had improved.

Only one group of Americans did not share in the colonies' freedom. Close to 500,000 people of African descent lived in North America at the time of Ben's birth. Most were slaves, working on farms and plantations in the southern colonies. Slavery existed in northern colonies too, and although many colonial leaders spoke out against the institution, the business of buying and selling humans was common.

Everyone living in the colonies was considered a British subject and owed allegiance to the king. The king created colonies and appointed governors. England also regulated trade and provided for defense. Beyond that, colonists ran their own affairs. They had their own legislatures, called assemblies, where elected officials passed laws and levied taxes.

Who voted for these officials?

In most colonies it was only men who owned property. (Women did not have the right to vote.) In the eighteenth century, however, property meant almost any valuable possession, such as an ax or musket. Because of this broad definition many men had a voice in local politics. At one town meeting one observer noted, "Each individual has an equal liberty of delivering his opinion, and is not liable to be silenced or browbeaten by a richer or greater townsman than himself, and each vote weighs equally whether that of the highest or lowest inhabitant."

Because of these freedoms, the colonies were already becoming a place of hope for those longing for a decent life, a place, Ben later reflected, where "every man is a freeholder, has a vote in public affairs [and] lives in a warm, tidy house. . . . Long may they continue in that situation."

When he was six, Ben moved with his parents, brother Thomas, and sisters Lydia, Jane, and Sarah to a house on the corner of Union and Hanover Streets. Three times the size of the cottage on Milk Street, the new house and its adjoining candle shop stood in the middle of the business district, next to the Green Dragon Tavern. Best of all, at least to Ben, was its closeness to water. Two hundred feet north

BEN'S CHILDHOOD HOME

was the Mill Pond, perfect for fishing and wading. And right in front was Mill Creek, a canal that flowed into Boston Harbor. From his bedroom window he could see the harbor with its wonder of sloops and ketches, its forest of towering masts, and its exotic goods like rum, tea, and spices from such far-off places as Guinea, Madagascar, and Brazil. Looking out, he daydreamed of joining a ship's crew and sailing off for parts unknown. He longed "to break loose and go to sea."

FAMILY LIFE

Ben was born into a big and busy family. He was the fifteenth of seventeen children, but most of his older brothers and sisters were already married, with homes and families of their own, when he was growing up.

Still, his mother had her hands full with nine-year-old James, seven-year-old Sarah, three-year-old Thomas, and, of course, baby Benny. Two years later she would give birth to Lydia and then her last child, Jane. When Abiah wasn't caring for her children, she spun wool, wove cloth, cooked, cleaned, sewed, kept her husband's account books, sang psalms, and taught the children their prayers.

Ben's father, Josiah, was busy too, with the hard, smelly work of making soap and candles. Every week, in a cloud of flies, Josiah gathered fat from the slaughterhouses. He hauled it home in a wheelbarrow, and melted it in huge wooden vats. Since his workshop adjoined the house, Ben's nose constantly wrinkled at the stench of rancid animal fat and hot, melted wax.

Josiah and Abiah raised their children in the ways of the "Congregational" or Puritan church—a strict religion that believed in hard work and simple prayer, and followed a set of rigid rules governing everything from the color of clothing to the activities of church members on Sunday. At the age of three Ben was taught the Lord's Prayer. Every morning and evening Josiah led his family in hour long prayer, and grace was said over every meal. The whole family attended church twice weekly—on Thursdays and Sundays—where little Ben was expected to sit ramrod straight and silent for up to four hours. An active boy, he considered this a "true hardship."

Despite the preaching and praying, the Franklins enjoyed what their daughter Jane remembered as a good life: "We were fed plentifully, made comfortable with fire and clothing, and had seldom any contention among us. . . . All was harmony."

Ben might have argued her last words. "I never developed a closeness with my siblings," he once admitted. He and his brother James bickered endlessly with each other. And Thomas mocked and teased Ben so often, Ben once retaliated by knocking him flat on his bottom. Angered by his son's behavior, Josiah handed out what Ben believed was the worst of all punishments—memorizing long passages from the Bible.

One day when Ben was nine, his older brother, Josiah Jr.,

THE FRANKLIN GANG		
*ELIZABETH	BORN	1678
*SAMUEL	BORN	1681
*HANNAH	BORN	1683
*JOSIAH JR.	BORN	1685
*ANNE	BORN	1687
*JOSEPH I	BORN	1688
	DIED IN INFANCY	
*JOSEPH II	BORN	1689
	DIED IN INFANCY	
JOHN	BORN	1690
PETER	BORN	1692
MARY	BORN	1694
JAMES	BORN	1697
SARAH	BORN	1699
EBENEZER	BORN	1701
	DIED	1703
THOMAS	BORN	1703
BENJAMIN	BORN	1706
LYDIA	BORN	1708
JANE	BORN	1712

*Indicates children of Josiah Franklin and his first wife, Anne, who died in 1690

returned home after ten years at sea. Abiah cooked a feast for the occasion, and all the Franklin children—from thirty-seven-year-old Elizabeth to three-year-old Jane—gathered around the big oak table. It would be the one and only time Ben would sit down with every one of his brothers and sisters.

A Speedy Prayer

Even though his parents raised him in a strict, religious household, Ben thought praying was boring and a waste of time, as shown by this story from his childhood, which was related years later by his grandson, William Temple Franklin:

Dr. Franklin, when a child, found the long graces used by his father before and after meal tedious. One day after the winter provisions had been salted, 'I think, Father, if you were to say Grace over the whole cask—once and for all—it would be a vast saving of time.'

At a time when surprisingly few people learned to swim, seven-year-old Ben taught himself, using a book called *The Art of Swimming*. Besides illustrating the basic strokes, it taught him a number of tricks, including how to dive, how to swim while holding one foot, and even how to clip his toenails while underwater.

Ben remained an avid swimmer for the

A page from the book that taught Ben how to swim

rest of his life. Years later, when living in London, he exhibited these skills in the Thames River for a cheering, clapping crowd of spectators. He taught several Englishmen to swim and even considered starting a "school for the instruction of swimming." Later when he founded a school in Philadelphia, he insisted swimming be part of the studies—an unheard-of idea in those days!

Ben annoys his family with the screechy sounds of a tin whistle.

When he was seven years old, something happened that Ben would remember all his life. One day some friends of his father's filled Ben's pockets with change. Merrily he headed to a toy shop. Along the way he saw a boy playing a whistle and, charmed by its sound, gave the boy all of his money for it. Then he tooted home—through the streets of Boston and through the rooms of his house on Union Street. But what was music to Ben's ears was nothing but noise to his family's. The high-pitched shriek caused the family dog to bark and his baby sister, Jane, to cry. Annoyed, family members asked how much he had paid for the irritating toy. When they learned Ben had given all his coins for it, they laughed and told him he had paid four times as much as it was worth. As Ben thought of all the other things he could have bought, the whistle lost its charm. He "cried with vexation," then stuffed the now worthless whistle into a trunk, never to be played again. It was, Ben later wrote, "a bitter lesson not forgotten." From this experience Ben made up an expression to describe most of life's troubles. They came from "giving too much for the whistle."

FUN WITH UNCLE BENJAMIN

When Ben was nine, his namesake, Uncle Benjamin, arrived in Boston from England. Old and eccentric, Uncle Ben hung around the house on Hanover Street composing silly rhymes, teaching Ben a form of shorthand he had invented, and telling family stories like this one.

Back in England, when ancestors of the Franklins still lived there, the family suffered through a time of religious persecution. But they refused to give up their Bible and instead taped it under a footstool. When an adult wished to read it, "he placed the stool on his knees upside down and turned the pages." One of the children stood at the door as lookout in case anyone was coming. If someone was, the stool was turned down again on its feet, where the Bible remained concealed and as secret as before.

COTTON MATHER was Boston's most important minister. From his church pulpit he preached fiery sermons on topics ranging from the evils of witchcraft to the importance of smallpox inoculation. He believed it was his job as a church leader to teach, lead, and inspire all Bostonians to live moral lives. One day Reverend Mather was following young Ben down a narrow passageway when he suddenly cried out, "Stoop! Stoop!"

Before Ben could understand what the reverend was hollering about, he thumped his young head on a low beam.

Reverend Mather was a man who never missed an opportunity to give advice, and as Ben sat rubbing his battered forehead the clergyman said, "You are young, and have the world before you. Stoop as you go through it, and you will miss many hard thumps."

Years later Ben said, "This advice, thus beat into my head, has frequently been of use to me."

Cotton Mather, who taught Ben an important lesson on life

The steepled building known as the Boston Grammar (Latin) School, where Ben began his formal education

Josiah hoped his youngest son would become a clergyman. Since clergymen needed to be well educated, Ben was enrolled in this school at the age of eight. He did well, rising quickly to the head of his class. But Ben's father changed his mind about his son's future. Training for the church, he claimed, was too expensive. Yet the school was free, charging only six shillings for "fire money" (money used for wood to heat the school)—and even that was waived if students could not afford it. So, what was Josiah's real problem? Many historians believe that although Ben qualified for the school when it came to intelligence and scholarship, his father knew the boy was not pious enough to become a minister. After only one year Ben was removed.

A picture of a colonial schoolroom similar to the one Ben attended

After leaving the Boston Grammar (Latin) School, Ben was sent to Mr. Brownell's School for Writing and Arithmetic. Located in Mr. Brownell's home, it taught boys and girls the basics of math and penmanship. "I learned to write a good hand," Ben later said, "but I failed arithmetic." After only one year, Josiah withdrew Ben—he felt his ten-year-old son was grown enough to work with him in the candlemaking shop. This year, plus the one spent at the Latin school, would be all the formal education Ben would ever receive.

F A T H E R   A N D   S O N

When he was ten years old, Ben and his friends decided to build a small wharf in a nearby salt marsh. Earlier Ben had spied a pile of stones meant for building a new house. That night after the workmen left, he and his friends carried the stones away and built their wharf. The next morning when the workmen discovered the theft, they were furious. "We were," Ben wrote, "discovered, complained of, and corrected by our fathers." Ben, however, didn't think he should be disciplined. He tried to explain the usefulness of the wharf. But his father refused to listen. "Nothing," said Mr. Franklin, "is useful that is not honest."

By the time Ben and his friends dragged all the stones back, he had learned two things: "Rocks can be twice as heavy on the return trip" and "Let other people's property alone."

This was only one of many lessons Ben learned from his father. He was, said Ben, "ingenious. He could draw prettily, was skilled a little in music . . . and had a mechanical genius with tools." But the senior Franklin's greatest strengths were his "sound understanding and solid judgment." Ben remembered how people squeezed around the Franklin dinner table to consult with his father about church or town affairs. At these times Mr. Franklin allowed Ben to remain at the table so he could listen and "improve his mind." So fascinated was Ben by these discussions, he often forgot to eat. Later he claimed the conversations taught him "what was good, just and prudent in the conduct of life."

Mr. Franklin devoted much time to his youngest son. When he realized twelve-year-old Ben detested making candles, he closed up shop and took his son for a long walk. Together they watched glazers, bricklayers, and blacksmiths at their work. All the while Mr. Franklin hoped and prayed that his boy would see a job that interested him.

Ben did not. But this experience, he claimed, was certainly of value. "It has been useful for me to have learned so much," he wrote later in life. "I am able to do some trifling jobs in the house . . . and to construct little machines for my experiments."

And What of Ben's Mom? Although Ben wrote at length about his father and his father's influence, he said very little about his mother. His autobiography includes only two lines about her. Still, by all accounts he was an affectionate son who, as an adult, wrote her weekly letters until her death.

My mother had an excellent constitution; she suckled all ten of her children. . . . a discreet and virtuous woman.

TITLE PAGE FROM BEN'S FAVORITE BOOK

THE
Pilgrim's Progress
FROM
THIS WORLD,
TO
That which is to come:
Delivered under the Similitude of a
DREAM
Wherein is Discovered,
The manner of his setting out,
His Dangerous Journey, and safe
Arrival at the Desired Country.

By *JOHN BUNYAN.*

The second Edition, with Additions.

I have used similitudes, Hosea 12. 10.

Licensed and Entred according to Order.

LONDON:
Printed for *Nath.Ponder,* at the Peacock
in the *Poultrey,* near *Cornhil,* 1678.

ONE DAY when he was eight years old, Ben found among his father's small stack of books a copy of *Pilgrim's Progress,* by John Bunyan. An avid reader, Ben eagerly opened the cover and was swept away by its story. Before this his reading had been limited to sermons, essays, and Bible verses. *Pilgrim's Progress,* however, was a dramatic story about a man named Christian who takes a perilous journey to the "Celestial City." Although *Pilgrim's Progress*'s themes were religious, it was the first book Ben ever read that included characters, dialogue, and an adventurous plot. "What a revelation," Ben later wrote, "to discover that the written word need not be dry and overblown." Until his dying day, *Pilgrim's Progress* remained Ben's "very . . . favorite book."

FRANKLIN THE PRINTER.

BEN WORKING THE PRESSES AS A PRINTER'S APPRENTICE

When Ben was twelve, his father decided he should learn the printing trade from his brother James, who had just established his own printing business in Boston. James needed a helper. Josiah encouraged him to take Ben as his apprentice. After all, Ben's arms were strong enough from swimming to work the heavy manual presses. His way with language would make him a good editor and proofreader. And he was a quick and enthusiastic learner. James agreed, but Ben still longed to become a sailor. Josiah—who did not legally need his son's approval for an apprenticeship—convinced Ben to sign a document typical of the day. In it Ben promised to work without pay until he was twenty-one years old. He also gave his word that while an apprentice he would not get married, play cards, drink alcohol, or attend the theater (activities that the Puritans thought were immoral). In return James would provide Ben with food, clothing, and a new suit on his twenty-first birthday.

For the next five years Ben learned the craft of printing. He soon became a fine printer—even better than his big brother.

A RIFT BETWEEN BROTHERS

Started in 1721 when Ben was fifteen, the *New England Courant* quickly became the most spirited and independent-thinking of Boston's four newspapers. In its pages James criticized the colony's government, as well as its leaders—a practice against the law at that time. To hide his true identity, James wrote these criticisms in the form of letters to the editor, which he then signed with pen names—"Timothy Turnstone," "Harry Meanwell," "Fanny Mournful." One morning, however, James found a real letter beneath the printshop door. It was signed "Silence Dogood," and the author claimed to be a middle-aged widow—a widow with lots of opinions. For six months Silence's letters kept coming, on subjects ranging from Harvard College to hoopskirts. And James gleefully published every one. Not until October 1722 did he discover the truth—their author was really his sixteen-year-old brother, Ben! James was furious. He vowed never again to publish anything Ben had written. But this vow was short lived. Just months later, after James printed his opinion that some religious leaders were no better than pirates, he was arrested and jailed. Worse, his newspaper was taken away. Forbidden to print the *Courant* under his own name, he decided to print it under Ben's.

In order to do this, James returned Ben's apprentice papers. This was necessary to show that Ben was a free man and able to publish a newspaper. Secretly, however, James gave Ben a new set of papers for the remainder of his apprentice term. The wily James wanted both an apprentice and a newspaper.

Ben signed these secret papers and began publishing the *Courant*. Under his direction the newspaper prospered. Circulation increased, its price was raised, and a new editorial policy was announced. "The main design of this weekly paper will be to entertain the town with the most comical and diverting incidents in human life," Ben printed on the paper's front page. He began to look with sharp, humorous eyes at the people and events around him. He began using his wit to record what he saw.

Ben quickly outgrew his apprentice posi-

tion. By the time James was ready to take back control of the newspaper, Ben had discovered he could manage on his own. One day, angered over a small mistake, James tried to hit his brother. Ben resisted. He said he was leaving. What could James do? No one else knew about the secret set of apprentice papers. Everyone thought Ben was a free man. If James made public their secret arrangement, he could end up back in jail. Still, he refused to let Ben leave on good terms. Bitterly he called on every printer in Boston and told them not to employ his brother. Since no one would offer Ben a job, James felt sure his brother would come crawling back.

But an advertisement placed in the *Courant* on September 16, 1723, tells a different story. The ad read: "James Franklin, printer in Queen's Street, wants a likely lad for an apprentice."

The newspaper where Ben apprenticed, founded by James Franklin

AN UNLIKELY BEGINNING

On a gloomy October morning in 1723 sixteen-year-old Ben crept from his house before dawn and slipped onto a ship bound for New York City. He was running away from a dreary apprenticeship, an abusive brother, and a city full of stifling rules. He hoped to find work in New York, but when he arrived, he learned there were no jobs for a printer. Try Philadelphia, someone suggested. Ben did. After an exhausting three-day trip by boat he landed in that city. This is how he described his first day:

> *I was in my working clothes, my best clothes being to come round by sea. I was dirty from my journey; my pockets were stuffed out with shirts and stockings and I knew no soul nor where to look for lodging. I was fatigued with traveling, and want of rest. I was very hungry, and my whole stock of cash consisted of a Dutch dollar and about a shilling in copper.*

B E N ' S   F I R S T   G L I M P S E   O F   P H I L A D E L P H I A ,   1 7 2 3

At the time, Philadelphia was the largest city in the American colonies—bigger than New York and Boston combined. It was also a merrier, more colorful city than Ben was used to. Unlike Boston's weathered-gray houses, Philadelphia's storefronts were painted red, blue, green, and yellow. Brightly painted carriages bounced over the muddy, rutted roads. The people were colorful too, with a taste for fine clothing and elaborate hairdos. Philadelphians loved parties and amusements, and enjoyed getting together to talk, sing, and eat. It was much different from prim, solemn Boston, and Ben loved it. From the moment he set foot on Market Street, he considered Philadelphia his "hometown."

Ben meets Deborah Read

With his spare socks and underwear stuffed into his pockets, and a loaf of bread stowed under each arm, Ben made quite a sight as he strolled down the street on his first day in Philadelphia. In one of the doorways a girl stood. She took one look at Ben and laughed out loud. Ben's cheeks burned with embarrassment. How infuriating to be laughed at— especially by a girl! Why, he would give her a piece of his mind if his mouth weren't full of bread. Instead he stomped off and hoped never to see her again. But his hopes were dashed the very next day when he rented a room. His landlord, as it turned out, was the girl's father, a shopkeeper named John Read. Ben found himself living under the same roof with her . . . and liking it! In the months that followed Ben and Deborah Read courted. They even spoke of marriage. But Ben wasn't ready to "take a wife" yet. It would be years before that same girl would become Deborah Franklin.

SIR WILLIAM KEITH
WHO SENT BEN TO LONDON

JUST ONE DAY after arriving in Philadelphia, Ben found work with Samuel Keimer, a printer described by Ben as "a mere compositor, knowing nothing of press work." Word of the young runaway employed in a local print-shop soon reached the ears of Sir William Keith, governor of Pennsylvania. Was the lad as fine a printer as people said? Governor Keith decided to find out. He visited Ben at work and took an instant liking to him. He offered to set Ben up in his own printing business, the funds for which would later be repaid "from the shop's profits." The governor sent Ben to London to buy the printing equipment. But when the young man arrived, he discovered Sir William had not sent along any money or letters of credit. Stranded and penniless in a foreign city, Ben learned the truth about Sir William: He was the type of man who liked to appear generous and often made promises he could not keep. Wrote Ben, "Sir William wished to please everybody, and having little to give, he gave expectations." Ben was furious. Sailing across the ocean, he had considered himself a man on the brink of success. Now he was simply an out-of-work teenager with no place to stay and no friends within three thousand miles.

THE INTERIOR OF AN EIGHTEENTH-CENTURY PRINT SHOP SIMILAR TO PALMER'S PRINTING HOUSE, LONDON, 1724

Alone and penniless in London, Ben did the only thing possible—he took his first of two printing jobs. It was in the city's largest and finest print shop, Palmer's, printing books, pamphlets, and government documents like stamps and paper money. For the next year and a half he set type and worked the presses. He learned so much that when he returned to Philadelphia, he was a far better printer than anyone else in the entire colony of Pennsylvania. "My time [at Palmer's] transformed me from a boy who knew a bit about printing, into a master printer," Ben later recalled.

No Meat for Ben

When he ran away from Boston, Ben was an ardent vegetarian. He believed eating an animal was a "kind of unprovoked murder." But while he was sailing to London, his shipmates caught and cooked some fish. Hungry and tired, Ben looked twice at both the fish and his beliefs.

I had formerly been a great lover of fish, and when this came hot out of the frying pan, it smelt admirable well. . . . I balanced some time between principle and inclination, till I recollected that when the fish were opened, I saw smaller fish taken out of their stomachs. Then, thought I, if you eat one another, I don't see why we mayn't eat you. . . . So convenient a thing it is to be reasonable creatures, since it enables one to find or make a reason for everything one has a mind to do.

BEN AND SOME PRINTERS SUPPING ON
"HOT-WATER GRUEL" AND BREAD

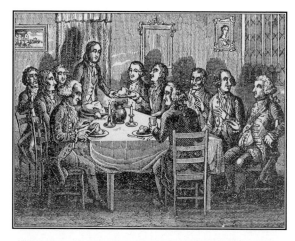

While in London, Ben took it upon himself to encourage his fellow workmen to "give up the cursed beverage, beer." It was common belief at the time that drinking strong beer made a person strong. But Ben believed differently. He noted that not only did beer-drinking printers "slosh around quite a bit," but the cost of the drink kept many of them in poverty. After Ben proved he was strong enough to carry a large form of type up and down the stairs without partaking of any morning beer, several of the men decided to give Ben's breakfast a try. They ate "a porringer of hot-water gruel sprinkled with pepper, crumpled with bread, and a bit of butter in it." Not only did the men save money, but Ben's breakfast "kept their heads clearer," too.

BEN BOARDS A SHIP BOUND FOR PHILADELPHIA.

In July 1726, after nineteen months in London, Ben headed home. His passage was paid by Thomas Denham, a wealthy Philadelphia merchant visiting England who'd met and taken pity on the homesick boy.

SHOPKEEPER OR PRINTER?

Back in Philadelphia, Ben worked as a clerk in Mr. Denham's general store. Intelligent and well spoken, Ben quickly became expert at selling. He also learned to stock shelves, keep books, and order goods. He began to see himself as a merchant. But fate saw things differently. Just months after their return Mr. Denham caught a cold and died. Jobless again, the twenty-one-year-old returned to the trade he knew best—printing. After borrowing money from the father of his friend Hugh Meredith, he opened his own shop on High Street. His first customer was a farmer looking for a place to get some printing done. Ben brought him into the shop, where he spent five shillings. "It was," Ben said, "the most wonderful money I had ever earned." Ben Franklin had found his way.

EARLIEST KNOWN PORTRAIT OF BEN, PAINTED AROUND 1738, SHOWS HIM AS THE SUCCESSFUL YOUNG MAN.

Ben's time in London did not diminish his ambition. Instead it was a reminder that a "young man who has chosen to strike his own way in the world can count on nothing but his own efforts and abilities." Ben worked hard when he returned to Philadelphia, and within fifteen years he was able to have this portrait painted. Wearing his best curled wig and ruffled finery, he wanted to look every inch the wealthy businessman. Since only prominent people sat for portraits in the eighteenth century, with this painting Ben was telling people that he had survived and prospered in Philadelphia. And he had done it "all on [his] own."

THE FAMILY ALBUM

A man with a large family . . . stands a broader mark for sorrow. But then, he stands a broader mark for pleasure too!

BENJAMIN FRANKLIN, LETTER TO BISHOP SHIPLEY, 1788

HUSBAND AND WIFE

A nineteenth-century woodcut shows Ben proposing to Deborah Read.

HE MET HER—that girl in the doorway—on the very day he arrived in Philadelphia. The two grew close. They fell in love. But their courtship was a rocky one. Ben sailed to England and did not return for eighteen months. While he was gone, Deborah married a potter named John Rogers. But Rogers made a poor husband. Not only was he a free spender, piling up mountains of debt, but it was rumored that he already had a wife in England. Disgusted, Deborah returned to her mother's house. And Rogers sailed for the West Indies. Soon, unconfirmed reports arrived from the Caribbean that Rogers had died. Could it be true? Was Deborah really a widow, free to marry again? Ben, recently returned from England, hoped so. "Our mutual affection was revived," he wrote, "and I took her to wife on September 1, 1730." But instead of recording the marriage in church, or celebrating in any way, Deborah simply came to live in Ben's house and began calling herself Mrs. Franklin. It was a common-law marriage—a perfectly acceptable practice in the eighteenth century. It also protected the couple from charges of bigamy—a crime punishable in the colony of Pennsylvania by thirty-nine lash strokes and life imprisonment.

Benjamin once wrote a song to Deborah. The name Joan simply refers to any woman, while the word "Joggy" is colonial slang for homely one. Included here are four of the original eight stanzas.

My Plain Country Joan

Of their Chloes and Phillisses poets may prate
I sing of my plain country Joan
Now twelve years my wife, still the joy of my life
Blest day that I made her my own,
My dear friends
Blest day that I made her my own.

Not a word of her face, her shape, or her eyes,
Of flames or of darts shall you hear;
Tho' I beauty admire t'is virtue I prize,
That fades not in seventy years,
My dear friends
That fades not in seventy years.

Some faults we all have, and so may my Joan,
But then they're exceedingly small;
And now I'm us'd to 'em, they're just like my own,
I scarcely can see 'em at all,
My dear friends,
I scarcely can see 'em at all.

Were the fairest young princess, with millions in purse
To be had in exchange for my Joan,
She could not be a better wife, might be worse,
So I'd stick to my Joggy alone
My dear friends
I'd stick to my Joggy alone.

ON BEING A HUSBAND

During the many years he was married, Ben stressed only his wife's good points, obviously taking his own advice:

Keep your eyes wide open before marriage, half-shut afterwards.

Deborah proved to be "a good and faithful helpmate," wrote Ben. "She cheerfully attended me in my business, folding and stitching pamphlets, tending shop, purchasing old linen rags for the paper makers, etc., etc." He also proudly recalled that in the early years of their marriage, when money was tight, he had been "clothed head to foot in woolen and linen of my wife's manufacture." But over the years Ben and Deborah slowly moved apart. As he grew into his role as a world-renowned writer, scientist, and statesman, she remained the shopkeeper's daughter—sharp tongued and given to fits of temper. More and more jealous of the time he gave to public affairs, she once told a friend, "All the world claims the privilege of troubling my Pappy," her pet name for Ben. When Ben sailed for England in 1757, Deborah wrote, "Now he is gone, I will not bear the least little thing in the world." For the next seventeen years the two lived on opposite sides of the Atlantic Ocean, and although Deborah pleaded with him to return— "When will it be in your power to come home? How I long to see you"— he did not come. During the winter of 1768–69 Deborah suffered a severe stroke that slurred her speech and erased her memory. A Philadelphia friend, Dr. Thomas Bond, wrote to Ben that "her constitution in general appears impaired. . . . these are bad

The only existing portrait of Deborah Franklin, painted when she was in her fifties

symptoms." Now the letters Deborah wrote to Ben often made no sense, her thoughts and sentences wandering and confused. Still Ben did not go home. Then in February 1775 he received a clipping from the *Pennsylvania Gazette.* It read: "On Monday, the 19th of December, died Mrs. Deborah Franklin, wife of Dr. Franklin." It was sad news for Ben. "I have lately lost my old and faithful companion," he later wrote, "and I every day become more sensible of the great loss which cannot be repaired."

F A T H E R   A N D   S O N

In late 1730 or early 1731 William "Billy" Franklin was born under mysterious circumstances. Despite Ben's resolve to lead a moral life, he had had a love affair with a woman whose identity he never revealed. His silence, however, did not keep people from gossiping. Was William actually Deborah's child, conceived before she and Ben were married, as some people speculated? Or was his mother really a servant named Barbara who worked in the Franklin household? The best clue comes from one of Ben's Philadelphia friends who wrote, "'Tis generally known here the child's birth is illegitimate and his mother not in good circumstances. I understand some small provision is made by [Ben] for her, but her being the most agreeable of women prevents particular notice being shown, or the father and son acknowledging any connection with her." Ben accepted full responsibility for the baby, and Deborah agreed to raise him as her own. She did so, however, grudgingly

B EN   T U T O R I N G   H I S
M U C H - L O V E D   F I R S T B O R N   S O N,
W I L L I A M

and with little affection. By the time William reached his teenage years, Deborah no longer bothered to hide her dislike of him. Mrs. Franklin, wrote one observer, went for days without taking any notice of her stepson. And when she did speak of him, she used the "foulest terms . . . ever heard from a gentlewoman." Luckily the treatment William received from

his father was much different. From the moment Billy entered the Franklin household, Ben lavished money and attention on him. Billy went to the finest schools. His books were specially ordered from London. He even owned a pony—a real extravagance in those days. And while his cousins apprenticed as goldsmiths or candlemakers, Ben had bigger plans for his "little Billy." He was going to be a gentleman. Such indulgence made the teenage William, as he later preferred to be called, a bit of a snob. Philadelphians described him as "a tall and proper youth . . . much of a beau." John Adams called him "a base born brat." Even Ben admitted to his sister Jane his fear that William had "acquired the habit of idleness." Still, he adored his son and would go to great lengths to make sure William's life was comfortable. "Everyone who knows me," Ben once said, "thinks I am too indulgent a parent."

P A R E N T A L   A D V I C E   F R O M   B E N

Ben gave this advice on child rearing:
Pray let [children] have everything they like; I think it of great consequence while the features are forming. It gives them a pleasant air, and that being once . . . fixed . . . the face is ever handsomer for it.

A 1769 PORTRAIT OF WILLIAM FRANKLIN, THE ROYAL GOVERNOR OF NEW JERSEY

Twenty-seven-year-old William went with his father to England in 1757. There he studied law and met the richest, most powerful men in the British Empire. Because of these connections, as well as Ben's influence, William was appointed by King George III to the position of royal governor of New Jersey. But as tensions between England and the colonies grew, so did the tensions between father and son. Ben became an ardent supporter of independence. William remained loyal to the king. Ben tried to persuade his son to join the patriots' side, but William did not think Americans could win the war, much less govern themselves. Besides, William did not like America and Americans as much as he liked England and her people. Angered by this attitude, Ben worked even harder to make the revolution succeed. He raised money and gave his own to the cause of the colonists. He wrote letters, reports, and resolutions, and helped with the important documents of a new nation. At the same time, William worked against the American cause. He sent secret letters to London filled with confidential information about the Continental Congress and its war plans. Eventually the New Jersey Assembly arrested him as a "virulent enemy to this country." But even this didn't stop William. After spending two years in a Connecticut jail, he headed to New York where he formed the "Associated Loyalists," a group that launched guerrilla attacks on American patriots. These actions deeply hurt Ben. It was bad enough his son stood against independence, but he was also fighting against his countrymen in the cruelest way, killing people from ambush and burning their homes and barns. Never again could Ben feel a father's love for William. In 1782, when he knew his cause was lost, William moved to London. He went without a single word of farewell from his father—the man with whom he had once shared such a close and loving relationship.

Heartache

After the Revolutionary War, William wrote these words from his home in London to Ben, who was in France:

How I desire to revive that affectionate intercourse and connection which till the commencement of the late troubles had been the pride and happiness of my life.... You must know I acted from a strong sense of what I conceived my duty to my King and ... my country. I verily believe that were the same circumstances to occur tomorrow, my conduct would be exactly similar.... All this, however, is history.... My fondest hope is to now resume our relationship as it was before.

Ben responded to William's letter with one of his own. In it he wrote:

Nothing has ever hurt me so much and affected me with such keen sensations as to find myself deserted in my old age by my own son; and not only deserted, but to find him taking up arms against me in a cause wherein my good fame, fortune, and life were all at stake.... there are natural duties which precede political ones, and cannot be extinguished by them.... This is a disagreeable subject. I drop it.... I shall be glad to see you when convenient, but would not have you come here [to France] at present.

In July 1785 the two met in Southampton, England, when Ben stopped there on his return to America. It was not the loving father-son reunion William had hoped for. William felt awkward and uncomfortable. Ben could not get over his anger. Two days later when the older Franklin sailed for Philadelphia, nothing had been resolved.

Afterward William disconsolately wrote this in his diary: "My fate has thrown me on a different side of the globe." Ben kept his feelings to himself. Father and son never saw each other again.

T H E   L O S T   S O N

BEN'S SECOND-BORN SON, FRANCIS FOLGER

In 1732 Deborah and Ben were blessed with a bright baby boy. From his birth little Franky was his mother's darling and his father's delight. Since the family still lived above the printshop, Franky often toddled after his father down the stairs and into the work area. His little eyes grew wide at the sight of the presses, the inking, the composing and cutting. Ben indulged the little boy and dreamed of the day Franky would take over the family business. But these dreams were dashed. In 1736 four-year-old Franky caught smallpox and died. Ben grieved deeply. For the rest of his life the sight of other boys reminded him of his loss. And fifty years later he still wept when he spoke of Franky. "I always thought he would be the best of my children . . . ," he said. "To this day I cannot think of him without a sigh."

F A T H E R   A N D   D A U G H T E R

SARAH, or Sally as she was called, made her appearance in the Franklin household just before electricity did, in 1743. Growing up, Sally often felt like an only child, since William was already a teenager when she was born. The house glowed, she claimed, with warmth, fun, and her father's pride. "My little Sally is the greatest lover of her books and school of any child I ever knew," Ben boasted. Along with reading and writing, Sally learned to knit and embroider. Ben even hired a tutor to teach her how to make buttonholes properly. But Sally's true love was music.

Ben sent her a harpsichord from England, and in years to come father and daughter discovered the joy of making music together—Sally on her harpsichord, Ben on the instrument he invented, the glass armonica. Unfortunately, Ben missed much of Sally's life. When he set sail for England in 1757, he said good-bye to a fourteen-year-old girl. When he returned, he found a "fair-haired, blue-eyed" wife and mother, "somewhat tending to plumpness." Sally never left home. She and her husband, Richard Bache, raised their seven children in the

The only existing portrait of Sarah Franklin, Ben's daughter

Franklins' big house on High Street. When Ben returned home for good, they "provided great ease and comfort" in his old age.

F A T H E R   O F   T H E   B R I D E

Sally married Richard Bache in October 1767. In England when it happened, Ben was furious at the news. Why, he fumed, would his socially prominent daughter link her life to a man who owned a dry-goods store? For a full year Ben refused to acknowledge the existence of his son-in-law. Then, unable to stay angry at his "baby girl," he wrote these words to Richard:

> *Loving Son,*
> *In this situation of my mind, you should not wonder that I did not answer your letters. I could say nothing agreeable; I did not choose to write what I thought, being unwilling to give pain where I could not give pleasure. Still, time has made my mind easier. If you prove a good husband and son, you will find in me an affectionate father.*

HOME SWEET HOME

HIGH STREET, THE FRANKLINS' PHILADELPHIA NEIGHBORHOOD

Ben and his family lived in three different homes during their Philadelphia years. The first, located above the printshop, was close to the market. But when Ben retired from the printing business in 1748 to focus on his electrical experiments, he moved his family from these rooms to a spacious house away from the noisy business district. Here the family remained until 1760, when Ben and Deborah built their third home—the home in which Deborah died in 1774 and in which Ben would not live until he returned from England the following year. Still, all these homes had one thing in common: They were located on the same busy street, then called High. (It is now Market Street.) Ben considered High Street his neighborhood, "close to the heart of things."

A nineteenth-century engraving of a colonial kitchen shows how the Franklins' second home may have looked.

Although there were only four Franklins— Ben, Deborah, William, and Sally— many others came to live with the family. Deborah's mother, the Widow Read, lived there until her death, supporting herself by making "a cure for the itch," which she sold at Ben's printshop. Various apprentices to Ben also stayed at the house, as well as nieces, nephews, and cousins. Surrounded by a wrought-iron fence, the two-story building included a study, a dining room, and Ben's "electrical laboratory," which attracted many guests. "Our home," Ben once wrote, "is full of comings and goings."

A NEWSPAPER ADVERTISEMENT SHOWS THE OUTSIDE OF BEN'S THIRD HOUSE.

In 1790 his grandson Benny used this newspaper ad: "To be Let—the Mansion House of the late Dr. Franklin." What do we know about this house? It had a large upstairs library and was lavishly decorated with the finest European wallpaper, furniture, and crystal. It was also built to be fireproof; "wood not touching wood," as Ben explained it. The house may have had one other unique characteristic. Historical evidence suggests it had indoor plumbing—a first in American history!

G R A N D P A P A   B E N

Temple, as Ben called him, was born in 1760 in London to William and an unknown woman. When William told Ben about the new baby, Ben wanted to bring it into the family. But William made a different decision. He placed his infant with a good family living in the country and for the next few years disguised his connection to the boy. Ben strongly disagreed with this decision. Still, he kept his opinion to himself. He visited Temple often and paid his bills, including the one for his education at a fine boarding school. When Ben returned to Pennsylvania in 1775, he took Temple with him. At fifteen, the boy was intelligent and handsome, with a gift for drawing and languages. He looked forward to seeing America and meeting his father, the royal governor of New Jersey. But Ben was worried. What if

PORTRAIT OF WILLIAM
TEMPLE FRANKLIN, BEN'S
OLDEST GRANDSON

William managed to turn Temple into a loyalist, faithful to the English crown? "It is enough that I have lost my son: would they add my grandson?" Ben asked. So he made a decision. When Congress sent him to France in 1776, he brought sixteen-year-old Temple along. The boy, Ben told Congress, would serve as his secretary. But Temple was not the best

choice for the job. A man about-town, he wore expensive brocade vests, attended all-night parties, slept until midafternoon, and ogled the French girls. He was, said one French acquaintance, "dependent on his grandfather's influence, and accomplished very little." After the Revolutionary War, Ben gave Temple, now in his late twenties, a farm in New Jersey. He felt sure this generous gift would settle him. But the young man quickly grew bored with country life and longed for the excitement of Europe. So Ben, overlooking all of Temple's flaws, tried to get him a diplomatic appointment abroad. He failed. Temple's reputation as a fop was too great. Temple remained in New Jersey until Ben died a few years later, still worrying about the fate of his most beloved grandson.

As an old man, returned from France, Ben finally had time to enjoy the "little prattlers," his nickname for his grandchildren. Born to daughter Sally and her husband, Richard Bache, they all lived in Ben's home. Besides teenage Benny, there were Willy, Betsy, Louis, Deborah, Richard, and the toddler, Sarah. "I am now in the bosom of my family, and find a batch of new babies who cling about the knees of their grandpapa, and afford me great pleasure," Ben wrote.

Ben sits in his Philadelphia garden surrounded by friends and grandchildren.

THE OTHER GRANDSON:
BENJAMIN FRANKLIN BACHE

When Benjamin Franklin Bache was born in 1769, he became the center of all attention. His parents, Sally and Richard, adored him. His grandmother Deborah nicknamed him "Kingbird," and told him stories about his famous grandpapa who was far away in England.

But things soon changed. Grandmother died, and no one called him Kingbird anymore. As revolutionary fever escalated, his friends started playing war games, marching in the streets and carrying toy guns. And his famous grandpapa returned from England with a teenage cousin no one had even known existed, named Temple.

Grandpapa and Temple spent an entire year in the Philadelphia house, and Benny's once-simple life turned topsy-turvy. Now there was a constant rush of visitors to the big house on High Street. His grandpapa hurried from meeting to meeting. Everyone hustled and bustled. Then one day Benny's mother told him he was going to sail across the ocean with Grandpapa and Temple, where he would get a European education. Benny had just turned seven.

"A special good boy," is how Ben described Benny a few days after the trio arrived in France, and after some consideration he decided to send his small grandson to school in Switzerland. Here Benny remained for the next four years, studying Latin and arithmetic. Was he homesick? Probably. But Benny was a "solemn and quiet boy" who did not express his unhappiness. Instead he wrote letters to Ben telling him about the magician he'd seen, or the birth of three guinea pigs in his room, or his first dance.

In 1782 Benny returned to Paris and his grandpapa. "I am determined to give him to a trade that he may have something to depend on," Ben wrote to the boy's father. Which trade? Printing, of course. He taught Benny about composing and inking, and sent for the best teachers in France. By the time Benny returned with his cousin and grandfather to America in 1785, he was an accomplished printer. After attending college, he was set up in his own printing house. "I have great pleasure in Ben," Grandpapa told a friend. "He is a good, honest lad and will make, I think, a valuable man."

Ben was right. Although his grandfather did not live to see it, Benny Bache went on to publish the *Aurora and General Advertiser,* which became the second-most-popular newspaper in Philadelphia after Ben's own *Pennsylvania Gazette.*

THE WRITER'S JOURNAL

> If you would not be forgotten, as soon as you are dead and rotten,
> either write things worth the reading, or do things worth the writing.
>
> —Benjamin Franklin, *POOR RICHARD'S ALMANACK*, 1738

Twelve-year-old Ben selling his own ballads on the streets of Boston

Ben first attempted to become a writer when he "took a fancy to poetry, and made some little pieces." One of these poems was a ballad about the famous pirate Edward Teach, better known as Blackbeard:

> Will you hear of a bloody battle,
> Lately fought upon the seas,
> It will make your ears to rattle,
> And your admiration cease:
> Have you heard of Teach the Rover,
> And his knavery on the Main;
> How of gold he was a lover,
> How he loved ill got gain.

He also wrote a ballad called "The Lighthouse Tragedy," about a family that drowned at sea. When Ben showed these pieces to his older brother, James was so impressed he printed them in little pamphlets and sent Ben around town to sell them. In those days original ballads were very popular and some men were able to sell enough to make their living at it. But Josiah told his son that verse makers were "generally beggars." So even though the ballads sold well, and it seemed he could avoid such a fate, Ben still followed his father's advice and gave up ballad writing.

THE SELF-TAUGHT WRITER

When he was twelve years old, Ben decided to become a better writer. There was at that time another boy in Boston, named John Collins, who also longed to improve his writing skills. The boys began exchanging letters and essays in which they tried to use good grammar, strong reasoning, and an advanced vocabulary. After several months, Ben thought he had become a fine writer. But one day, Josiah found copies of the papers Ben had sent to his friend. After reading them, he pointed out that Ben spelled and punctuated better than John. But, he said, Ben "fell far short in elegance of expression and manner."

Ben took his father's criticism to heart. He promised to improve his writing style and figured out a way to do it. At that time an excellent newspaper called the *Spectator* was published in England. It had greatly influenced many writers with its simple and elegant style. Ben began reading every word of it. He jotted down ideas from its articles, then put the ideas away. After a few days he rewrote the ideas in his own words. He then compared his sentences with the *Spectator*'s. When he found faults, he corrected them.

He soon realized he needed to improve his vocabulary as well. What to do about this? Ben decided to write everything in rhyme. In this way he forced himself to learn new words that fit the rhyme but still made sense. After writing a suitable rhyme, he turned it all around and rewrote the whole piece in prose. He did this over and over again, late into the nights and even on weekends. Eventually his hard work paid off. "Around the age of sixteen I began to think," Ben said, "that I would make a tolerable writer."

Ben's Rules for Being a Better Writer

Everyone, Ben believed, had a need to communicate well. Over the years he developed and stuck to these writing rules.

Good writing should be smooth, clear and short, and the art of saying little in much must be avoided at all costs. In written discourse, every needless thing gives offense and must be eliminated. . . . Had this always been done, many large and tiresome volumes would have shrunk into pamphlets, and many a pamphlet into a single period.

The printing press Ben used to publish his newspapers, pamphlets, and almanacs

How did it work? First Ben arranged cast-metal letters into words, sentences, and paragraphs that would become the lines of printed text. These lines were held in place by a wooden case, or frame, called the composing stick. Next he slathered the type with an even layer of ink and laid a sheet of white paper on top. He then pulled down a bar that pressed the inky, wet type and the sheet of white paper together. After the bar was released, the paper was removed and hung over wooden rods to dry. It was, as Ben once said, a "tediously slow process." In order to print three thousand copies of his weekly newspaper, the *Gazette,* Ben had to repeat every one of the above actions three thousand times. It is no wonder he often worked through the night in order to get all his printing done.

BEN OUTSIDE THE DOOR OF HIS PRINTING SHOP ON HIGH STREET

THE ATMOSPHERE in Ben's tiny, ink-scented shop was one of excitement, for in early America a printing shop was the center of news and opinions. While Ben busied himself gathering the news, writing articles and almanacs, and printing pamphlets, books, and papers, his wife, Deborah, minded the stationery store, where the Franklins sold ink, quills, and paper; spectacles, books, and sealing wax; Rhode Island cheese, mackerel by the barrel, and white stockings, among other items. Customers could also find the good Crown soap made by the Franklins back in Boston and "a cure for the itch," developed by Deborah's mother.

BEN BECOMES A NEWSPAPERMAN AT THE AGE OF TWENTY-THREE

Philadelphia already had two newspapers when Ben's *Pennsylvania Gazette* made its appearance in 1729. But from the moment readers picked it up, they knew that this newspaper was different. The *Gazette's* slogan advertised "the freshest advices [news] foreign and domestick." Some of its articles were indeed fresh—straight out of Ben's imagination: "They tell us in Wiltshire a man aged 66 was married to a maid of 26. . . . The match being made on Wednesday, they were married on Thursday, and the man died Friday. So the bride was courted, married, became a wife and a widow all within twenty-four hours."

The *Gazette* hired no help. Ben was reporter, editor, typesetter, circulation man, and business manager. To gather news, he asked his readers to tell him about any remarkable happenings. From New York, Ben reported, there had been news of terrible thunder and lightning, but no damage was done. "That same day," the report continued, "in Bucks county there was reported such terrible thunderstorms that one flash came so near a lad as to melt the pewter buttons right off his breeches. . . . 'Tis well nothing else thereabouts was made of pewter." Such refreshing nonsense was used sparingly, sneaked in between the real news of fires and robberies. And readers obviously loved it. Within a few short years the *Gazette* grew to become the largest newspaper in America, with distribution from New York to Virginia. But Ben stopped running the newspaper in 1748, deciding to pursue his scientific interests. The *Gazette,* however, continued to be published and was still under the editorship of his nephew when Ben died in 1790.

The first issue of the Pennsylvania Gazette.

A MAN OF LETTERS

Throughout his long life Ben wrote thousands of letters to his many friends, relatives, and business associates. Always full of amusing tidbits or beautifully expressed sentiments, they became popular in the colonies. It was common for a recipient of a Ben Franklin letter to share it; letters were copied, reprinted in newspapers, and passed from hand to hand. Sometimes people even stopped Ben on the street to ask for a copy of a letter he had sent to someone else. Ben obligingly wrote out their requests from memory. Below are four of Ben's most popular letters.

TO MISS GEORGINA SHIPLEY

On the loss of her American squirrel, which, escaping from its cage, was killed by a shepherd's dog

London, 26th September, 1772

Dear Miss: I lament with you most sincerely the unfortunate end of poor Mungo. Few squirrels were better accomplished, for he had a good education, had traveled far, and seen much of the world. As he had the honor of being, for his virtues, your favorite, he should not go, like common skuggs, without an elegy or epitaph. Let us give him one in monumental style and measure. . . .

EPITAPH
Here Skugg
Lies snug
As a bug
In a rug.

If you wish it, I shall procure another to succeed him; but perhaps you will now choose some other amusement.

Remember me affectionately to all the good family, and believe me ever your affectionate friend,
B. Franklin

TO DEBORAH FRANKLIN

While traveling to western Pennsylvania to build a fort

Gnadenhutten, 25th January, 1756

My dear child: This day we arrived here. I wrote to you the same day and once since. We all continue well, thanks be to God. . . . As to our lodging, 'tis on deal feather-beds, in warm blankets, and much more comfortable than when we lodged at our inn the first night after we left home; for the

woman being about to put very damp sheets on the bed, we desired her to air them first; half an hour afterward she told us the bed was ready and the sheets well aired. I got into bed, but jumped out immediately, finding them as cold as death and partly frozen. She had aired them indeed, but it was out upon the hedge! I was forced to wrap myself up in my great-coat and woolen trousers. Everything else about the bed was shockingly dirty.

As I hope in a little time to be with you, and my family, and chat things over, I now only add that I am, dear Debby,
Your affectionate husband,
B. Franklin

TO MRS. HUBBARD

On the death of Ben's brother John Franklin

Philadelphia, 23rd February, 1756

I condole with you. We have lost a most dear and valuable relation. But it is the will of God and nature that these mortal bodies be laid aside when the soul is to enter into real life. This is rather an embryo state, a preparation for living. A man is not completely born until he is dead. Why, then, should we grieve that a new child is born among the immortals, a new member added to their happy society?

Our friend and we were invited abroad a party of pleasure which is to last forever. His chair was ready first and he is gone before us. We could not all conveniently start together, and why should you and I be grieved at this, since we are soon to follow and know where to find him? Adieu,
B. Franklin

TO WILLIAM STRAHAN

At the beginning of the conflict between England and the American colonies

Philadelphia, July 5, 1775

Mr. Strahan: You are a member of Parliament, and one of that majority which has doomed my country to destruction. You have begun to burn our towns and murder our people. Look upon your hands! They are stained with the blood of your relations! You and I were friends. You are now my enemy, and I am
Yours,
B. Franklin

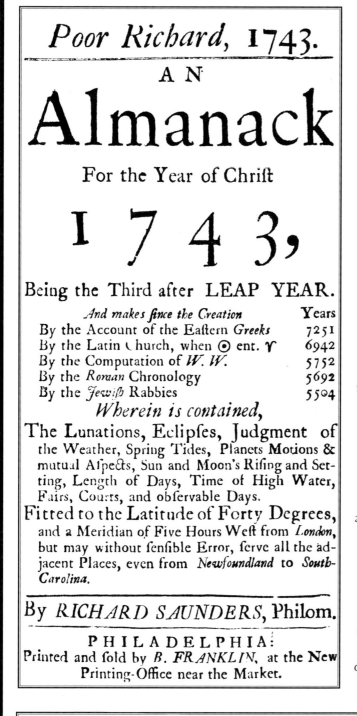

Poor Richard, 1743.

AN

Almanack

For the Year of Chrift

1 7 4 3,

Being the Third after LEAP YEAR.

And makes fince the Creation   **Years**
By the Account of the Eaftern *Greeks*   7251
By the Latin Church, when ☉ ent. ♈   6942
By the Computation of *W. W.*   5752
By the *Roman* Chronology   5692
By the *Jewifh* Rabbies   5504

Wherein is contained,

The Lunations, Eclipfes, Judgment of the Weather, Spring Tides, Planets Motions & mutual Afpects, Sun and Moon's Rifing and Setting, Length of Days, Time of High Water, Fairs, Courts, and obfervable Days.

Fitted to the Latitude of Forty Degrees, and a Meridian of Five Hours Weft from *London,* but may without fenfible Error, ferve all the adjacent Places, even from *Newfoundland* to *South-Carolina.*

By *RICHARD SAUNDERS,* Philom.

PHILADELPHIA:
Printed and fold by *B. FRANKLIN,* at the New Printing-Office near the Market.

THE COVER OF POOR RICHARD'S ALMANACK, 1743

Almanacs were a favorite form of reading in colonial America. Pocket-size books, they forecast weather and told about the tide and changes in the moon. At one time or another almost every printer in the colonies produced an almanac—hundreds of versions were on the market. And sales were extraordinary, outstripping all other books of the time combined. In December 1732, hoping to make some money, Ben decided to try his hand at publishing an almanac . . . but his would be different. Besides forecasts, he included jokes, riddles, and poems. Calling it *Poor Richard's Almanack,* a name he borrowed and adapted (without asking!) from *Poor Robin's Almanack,* which his brother James was publishing, Ben's book was both useful and funny. It was also wise, saucy, clever, and sometimes even vulgar. It encouraged poor colonists to work and save, but it also brought badly needed relaxation and laughter. And it became a colonial bestseller. Published once a year from 1732 to 1758, *Poor Richard's Almanack* was the most widely read book in America after the Bible. And because one out of every one hundred colonists bought it, at a price of two shillings per dozen, it turned Ben Franklin into a very wealthy man.

P O O R   R I C H A R D   B E G I N S

Poor Richard's Almanack first appeared in December 1732. From its opening words readers knew this almanac was different. Each edition was introduced by "Poor Richard Saunders." Who was he? Why, Ben Franklin, of course.

I might attempt to gain thy favor by declaring that I write almanacs for no other reason than that of the public good; but in that I would not be sincere. . . . The plain truth of the matter is, I am excessive poor, and my wife, good woman, is excessive proud; she cannot bear, she says, to sit spinning . . . while I do nothing but gaze at the stars. She has threatened to burn all my books and rattling-traps (as she calls my instruments) if I do not make some use of them for the good of my family. . . . I have thus begun to comply with my dame's desire.

Poor Richard's Almanack was sprinkled with memorable proverbs such as these, included in a later, illustrated version.

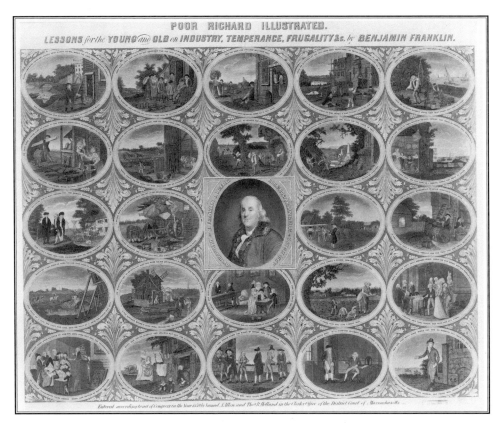

POOR RICHARD ILLUSTRATED.
LESSONS for the YOUNG and OLD on INDUSTRY, TEMPERANCE, FRUGALITY &c. by BENJAMIN FRANKLIN.

Ben stuffed hundreds of wise and witty sayings between weather forecasts and eclipse reports. As he told his readers, "These are scraps from the table of wisdom that will, if well digested, yield strong nourishment to the mind." Some he wrote himself, others he borrowed from the Bible, famous philosophers, and ancient writers. He then rewrote them to make them clear and simple for his colonial readership. They became known as the maxims of Poor Richard. His philosophy was expressed in such sayings as:

> There are no gains without pains.
> A penny saved is a penny earned.

God helps those who help themselves.

These words of wisdom helped mold the American character of hard work, common sense, and self-sufficiency. Ben preached them in all twenty-five annual editions of his almanac. But he never took them too seriously, as this maxim from the 1750 almanac proves:

> Who is wise? He that learns from everyone.
> Who is powerful? He that governs his passion.
> Who is rich? He that is content.
> Who is that? Nobody.

POOR RICHARD SAYS SOME NAUGHTY THINGS

Not all the maxims found in *Poor Richard's Almanack* were uplifting and instructive; some were downright racy. As Ben warned his readers, "Be not disturbed, O grave and serious reader, if among the many serious sentences in my book, thou findest the occasional pickle."

He that is conscious of a stink in his breeches, is jealous of every wrinkle in another's nose.

Three may keep a secret if two are dead.

Fish and visitors stink in 3 days.

He who lies down with dogs, gets up with fleas.

Love your neighbor, but don't pull down your hedge.

Sally laughs at everything you say. Why? Because she has fine teeth.

The ANATOMY of Man's Body, as governed by the Twelve CONSTELLATIONS.

♈ The Head and Face.

♊ Arms

♌ Heart

♎ Reins

♐ Thighs

♒ Legs

♉ Neck

♋ Breast

♍ Bowels

♏ Secrets

♑ Knees

♓ The Feet.

To know where the Sign is

Firſt Find the Day of the Month, and againſt the Day you have the Sign or place of the Moon in the 6th Column. Then finding the Sign here, it ſhews the part of the Body it governs.

The Names and Characters of the Seven Planets

☉ Sol, ♄ Saturn, ♃ Jupiter, ♂ Mars, ♀ Venus, ☿ Mercury, ☽ Luna, ☊ Dragon's head, and ☋ tail.

The Five Aſpects.

☌ Conjunction,   ☍ Oppoſition,   ✱ Sextile,
△ Trine,   □ Quartile.

A TONGUE-IN-CHEEK CHART BEN CREATED FOR HIS ALMANAC

Astrology was an important ingredient in most almanacs, including Ben's. Readers enjoyed having their "stars read and interpreted," and some believed that Poor Richard could predict future events. Wrote Ben, "Visitors pelted me with a thousand trifling questions. Will my ship return safe? Will my mare win the race? When will my wife die? When is the best time to cut my hair? Silly questions! I have had enough of 'em." In response to such queries Ben created an equally silly chart in which each body part was associated with a sign of the zodiac (the two arms with Gemini, the heart with Leo, the bowels with Virgo, and so on). After determining which of their own body parts was influenced by the stars and planets, Ben claimed, readers could predict their future from the function of that body part. Aches? Palpitations? Diarrhea? All could be signs from the cosmos.

Cover of one of the first magazines published in America . . . established by Ben

Looking for still other ways to expand his writing and printing business, Ben decided in 1740 to form a magazine. Modeling it on the *Gentleman's Magazine,* a popular London publication, he called it *The General Magazine and Historical Chronicle for All British Plantations in America,* nicknamed simply *The General Magazine.* He planned to examine politics and literature within its pages. But colonial Americans were not ready for such cultivated reading material. They did not subscribe, and within six months the publication folded.

A BROADSIDE, PRINTED IN 1785, OF ONE OF BEN'S BEST-KNOWN PIECES OF WRITING, "THE WAY TO WEALTH," OR "FATHER ABRAHAM'S SPEECH"

IN 1757 Ben skimmed through twenty-five years of his almanacs and pulled out all the maxims dealing with saving, earning, making, or investing money. He then worked them into a brief story about a fictitious character called Father Abraham, who had been a faithful follower of *Poor Richard's Almanack* for a quarter of a century. The story's tone was highly ironic and at times close to parody. Ben was actually laughing at himself and Poor Richard and the whole notion of persuading men to save money—while at the same time squeezing in as many quotations from his previous almanacs as he possibly could. The result was a story that was often difficult to read, as this passage shows:

> *Industry need not wish,* as Poor Richard says, and *he that lives upon hope will die fasting. There are no gains without pains*; then *help hands, for I have no lands,* or if I have, they are smartly taxed. And as Poor Richard likewise observes, *he that hath a trade hath an estate,* and *he that hath a calling hath an office of profit and honor.*

Still, when the story appeared in the 1758 almanac, readers loved it. They understood Ben was poking fun at himself

and at them, and it made them laugh. In fact, Ben's readers found the story so entertaining that it was later published separately as "Father Abraham's Speech." Under that title and its later title, "The Way to Wealth," it spread throughout the colonies and Europe, where it was translated into French, German, and Italian. Not only did it make Ben a famous author worldwide, it forever linked his name with the ideals of frugality and industry.

The first page of Ben's best-known bagatelle, "Dialogue Between Franklin and the Gout," with handwritten corrections by Madame Brillon

In 1778, while he was in France, Ben wrote a collection of funny essays and anecdotes. They were called bagatelles (meaning "trifles, little bits of fluff"), and were meant to entertain his French friends. "Dialogue Between Franklin and the Gout" was written when Ben succumbed to a two-week attack of that disease. A metabolic illness sometimes brought on by overeating, gout causes severe pain and joint inflammation, and Ben's had left him bedridden and depressed. To cheer himself up he wrote about the thing most on his mind—the gout. In his story Madame Gout scolds Ben for sitting and playing chess for hours, and riding in the coach instead of walking. When Ben grows bored of her lecture, Madame Gout responds, "I stand corrected. I will be silent and do my duty. Take this twinge—and that!"

"O! O-oo!" screams Ben. "Talk on, I pray you!"

Ben sent a copy to his friend Madame Brillon, who made suggestions for improvement. The story was then printed and circulated among Ben's many friends. Said one French courtier after reading it, "Dr. Franklin wields his wits like a sword."

FART PROUDLY

Because of its subject this essay by Ben doesn't often appear in his life story. Written in 1781, it poked fun at the Royal Academy of Brussels. Every year the academy posed a scientific question and gave a prize to the scientist who could figure out the answer. Ben thought the questions stuffy, pompous, and of little practical use, so he proposed his own. Could the academy's scientists discover a drug that, when mixed with food, would remove the disagreeable odor of "human digestive gasses"? The prize for such a discovery, Ben said, would be the gratitude of the entire world—far better than a "golden trophy."

> What comfort can [science] be to a man who has whirlwinds in his bowels? . . . Imagine the ease and comfort every man living might feel . . . by discharging freely the wind from his bowels. Especially if it be converted into perfume. . . . Think of the generous host who now may offer his guests the choice of claret or champagne, . . . then inquire whether they choose a musk, or lily, or wild rose scented drug to perfume their bodily odors. Surely such liberty of *ex-pressing* one's *scent-iments* . . . is infinitely more importance than a mathematical prize question. Indeed, such prizes, when compared to the happiness of a man who may fart proudly are hardly worth a *fart-hing*!

A HANDWRITTEN PAGE FROM BEN'S AUTOBIOGRAPHY

Every evening in the summer of 1771 in the tiny English village of Twyford the five lively daughters of Jonathan Shipley gathered with their parents to listen to the pages their guest had written that day. Sixty-five-year-old Ben Franklin was working on the story of his life, in the form of a long letter to his son, William. Presenting his life as a model for success, Ben's letter was entertaining—but it would remain unfinished. As the conflict with England grew he was forced to put aside his manuscript to deal with matters of war and independence. The autobiography was in his Philadelphia home in 1777 when the British occupied that city and commandeered Ben's house for their army headquarters. In the confusion the manuscript was thrown away. But luck was on Ben's side. An old friend spied the crumpled papers in the gutter, recognized the handwriting, and returned the letter to Ben. Not until 1784 did Ben again work on his autobiography, and from then on he only picked at it. The book takes readers only as far as Ben's first mission to England in 1757. Still, his unfinished book remains one of the most popular pieces of early American literature and is widely read even now.

A FRANKLIN FABLE

Ben often wrote stories to make a point. When England began mistreating the colonists and refused to treat them with the respect Ben felt they deserved, he wrote this fable:

> A lion's [cub] was put on board a ship bound to America as a present to a friend. . . . It was a tame and harmless kitten, and therefore [was allowed] to walk about the ship at pleasure. A stately, full-grown English Mastiff belonging to the captain, despising the cub's weakness, often took its food by force and turned it out of its [bed] when he had a mind to rest there himself. The young lion nevertheless grew daily in size and strength, and the voyage being long, soon became a more equal match for the mastiff; who, continuing his insults, received a stunning blow from the lion's paw that fetched his skin over his ears, and deterred him from any future show of strength. Poor mastiff! For the rest of the journey, he wished he had secured the lion's friendship, rather than provoked its anger.

Noah Webster, Ben's last writer friend

Ben was in his eighties when he became interested in the work of Noah Webster, who had just published a book on grammar. After reading the book, Ben wrote him a letter commending him on his "zeal for preserving the purity of our language," and expressing his hope that Webster would one day become "the authority on word usage, and spelling." Ben even suggested they get together and discuss a few ideas he had about the usage of nouns and verbs. Sadly, Ben was too old to do much work with Webster. He died just months later. Webster, however, went on to fulfill Ben's hopes. When he published his dictionary, he dedicated the first edition to Ben Franklin.

BEN DOING ONE OF THE THINGS HE LOVED BEST—WRITING

During his long life Ben wrote and published hundreds of articles, essays, almanacs, pamphlets, et cetera. He loved satires and early on directed them at the foolishness of people. Later, when he became involved in the colonies' fight for independence, he turned his sharp pen on the pomposity of the British Parliament. He liked witty writing and believed that humor was the hardest skill for any author to learn. Ben, however, had a hard time writing seriously, as his only attempt at composing a prayer proves:

> From a cross neighbor, and a sullen wife,
> A pointless needle and a broken knife;
> From suretyship, and from an empty purse,
> A smoky chimney, and a jolting horse;
> From a dull razor, and an aching head,
> From a bad conscience, and a buggy bed;
> A blow upon the elbow, and the knee,
> From each of these, Good Lord,
> Deliver me.

But funny or not, Ben always wrote honestly about the important issues of the day. He wasn't afraid to use strong words, to be bawdy or vulgar, or to play tricks on his readers if it helped make his point. "Writers," Ben once declared, "are the heroes of a society."

TOKENS OF A WELL-LIVED LIFE

The best service to God, is doing good to man.

—BENJAMIN FRANKLIN, 1784 LETTER TO MADAME BRILLON

Portrait of Ben—the middle-aged good citizen

Ben strongly believed in community service. From the moment he first came to Philadelphia in 1723, he had noticed things that needed to be done for the good of everyone. From fire departments to medical care to public education, Ben found ways to make improvements. By helping your fellow citizen, he claimed, you "not only improved mankind, but yourself as a man."

WHAT GOOD SHALL I DO TODAY?

All his life Ben tried to do what was right. His daily routine reminded him to put mankind's problems before his own.

I rose at five each morning, and addressed Powerful Goodness [Ben's name for God] with the same daily question: What Good Shall I Do Today? I then studied and planned my day until eight, worked until twelve, dined and overlooked my account books until two, worked again until six when I had supper, music and conversation. At ten I examined my day. What Good Had I Done That Day?

PROJECT PERFECTION

While trying to improve his community, Ben also tried to improve himself. When he was twenty-seven years old, he decided to become perfect. "I wished to live," he later wrote, "without committing any fault at any time." To achieve this goal he wrote down the following list of virtues and how to live by them:

1. Temperance. Eat not to dullness. Drink not to elevation.
2. Silence. Speak not but what may benefit others or yourself. Avoid trifling conversation.
3. Order. Let all things have their places. Let each part of your business have its time.
4. Resolution. Resolve to perform what you ought. Perform without fail what you resolve.
5. Frugality. Make no expense but to do good to others or yourself: i.e. waste nothing.
6. Industry. Lose no time. Be always employed in something useful.
7. Sincerity. Use no hurtful deceit. Think innocently and justly; and, if you speak, speak accordingly.
8. Justice. Wrong none, by doing injuries or omitting the benefits that are your duty.
9. Moderation. Avoid extremes. Forbear resenting injuries so much as you think they deserve.
10. Tranquility. Be not disturbed at trifles, or at accidents, common or unavoidable.
11. Cleanliness. Tolerate no uncleanness in body, clothes or habitation.
12. Chastity. Rarely use venery but for health or offspring.
13. Humility. Imitate Jesus and Socrates.

Always the scientist, Ben set up a tabulation system in a small notebook. He then proceeded to practice each virtue systematically, one each week. When the thirteen-week cycle ended, he began again. And at first he believed his approach to perfection was actually working. But the truth soon set in. "I had undertaken a task more difficult than I had imagined," Ben wrote. "While my care was employed in guarding against one fault, I was often surprised by another."

What was the virtue Ben had the most difficulty with? Order. "With regards to places for things, papers, etc., I am a dismal failure," he moaned. His friends and family agreed. John Adams, later to become the second president of the United States, recalled that Ben's belongings were "an appalling muddle."

Perfection, Ben eventually decided, was impossible to achieve. Still, he carried his virtue notebook with him the rest of his life. At the age of seventy-eight, while America's ambassador to France, he drew it from his pocket to show to a group of friends. The little book made such an impression one French admirer gushed, "We touched his precious booklet! We held it in our hand! Here was . . . the story of Franklin's soul."

AN EIGHTEENTH-
CENTURY ADVERTISING
CARD SHOWS THE
JUNTO AND ITS TWO
MAIN PURPOSES—
SOCIALIZING AND
SELF-IMPROVEMENT.

As a young businessman in 1727, Ben was so hungry for friendship and intelligent conversation, he formed a club with ten of his "cleverest acquaintances." Called the Junto (from the Spanish word *junta,* meaning "meeting"), the club met Friday nights at a nearby alehouse. There members read books, debated politics, discussed morals, posed intellectual questions, and drank beer. Each pledged to have "an inquiring spirit" and declared his "love for mankind." As the Junto grew in popularity Ben suggested each original member form a subordinate club, resulting in five or six new clubs. Ben used the Junto to influence opinion and promote public projects, such as the formation of a volunteer fire department and the opening of a library. The club lasted forty years and was, Ben thought, "the best school of philosophy, morality, and politics that ever existed in the province."

Ben (standing in the center of the room) and his fellow Junto members open the first subscription library in Philadelphia.

At Ben's suggestion members of the Junto gathered their books into a collection that was housed in their headquarters. The fledgling library was successful at first. But Junto members soon began to complain about the deteriorating condition of their books. So Ben suggested something totally different—a subscription library that would be open to the public! At that time private libraries were common enough among wealthy men, as were institutional libraries found in churches or colleges. But no one had ever begun a library for the public good. It was an unheard-of idea, one the Junto enthusiastically supported. Ben and other members soon began collecting subscriptions from Philadelphians. They asked for an initiation fee of forty shillings and annual dues of ten shillings per year (ironically, this was an amount average citizens could not afford). This money went toward purchasing books, and later toward renting a room large enough to house the ever growing collection. By 1742 the library contained more than three hundred volumes on science, theology, and history, among other subjects. Open from two until three on Wednesday afternoons, and from ten until four on Saturdays, it allowed "any civil gentleperson" to read the books in-house. Only subscribers, however, could borrow them, one volume at a time. Said Ben, "Reading became quite fashionable and our people in a few years were observed by strangers to be better informed and more intelligent than people of the same rank generally are in other countries." Called the Library Company of Philadelphia, it served as a model for introducing other libraries across the colonies. Ben's library still exists today in Philadelphia and contains some of its original collection, such as Homer's *Iliad* and *Odyssey,* Daniel Defoe's *The Complete English Tradesman,* and Sir Isaac Newton's *Principia.*

HIRING LAMPLIGHTERS, LIKE THIS ONE, WAS PART OF BEN'S STREET AND SANITATION PLAN.

Around 1736 Ben noticed the rutted, muddy state of Philadelphia's streets. He started talking to people and writing editorials in his newspapers. He convinced Philadelphians to pay for having the streets paved. But it wasn't enough. Noticing the garbage in the gutters, Ben convinced citizens to hire someone to pick up the trash and someone else to sweep the dust from the streets. Now things looked spick-and-span. But at night the city's badly designed streetlights kept everything in the dark. So Ben invented new ones that used four small panes of glass instead of a globe so that the top was open. This shape allowed the smoke from the candlelit lamps to rise instead of being trapped inside the glass. In this way the glass stayed cleaner and the lamps shone brighter. Who would take care of these new lamps? Ben suggested a well-disciplined staff of ladder-toting lamplighters. Soon they were making their regular rounds at twilight, and Philadelphia's streets were the envy of cities the world over.

BEN STARTS PHILADELPHIA'S FIRST VOLUNTEER FIRE DEPARTMENT

Without water systems, fire engines, or a hook-and-ladder wagon, a fire in Philadelphia could have been devastating. This worried Ben, so in 1736 he organized the Union Fire Company, basing his plan on one he had seen while in London ten years earlier. There, clubs of active men had been formed to combat fire. Each club owned its own horse-drawn fire engine and practiced with it regularly; included specialists who knew how to handle special equipment like axes and hooks; and had an officer who led the group and directed citizens in times of emergency. Duplicating the London model, the first volunteer fire department in Philadelphia had thirty members who were trained in both putting out fires and rescuing people. The company voted Ben as its chief. It also held monthly meetings for discussing new ideas about fire prevention. Ben had plenty of those. In his newspaper, the *Pennsylvania Gazette,* he printed suggestions, like removing wooden moldings from the sides of fireplaces, cleaning chimneys frequently, and tightly closing the lid of a bed warmer when it was filled with hot coals. Eventually, so many men volunteered that the first company grew too big, and soon Philadelphia had a network of well-trained, dedicated fire companies.

A middle-aged Ben wearing his volunteer fireman hat

EXTERIOR OF THE AMERICAN PHILOSOPHICAL SOCIETY, BEN'S
BRAINCHILD FOR PROMOTING SCIENCE ACROSS ALL THIRTEEN COLONIES.

IN 1743 BEN WROTE, "The first drudgery of settling new colonies is now pretty well over, and there are many in every province ready . . . to cultivate the finer arts and improve the stock of knowledge. . . . I propose that one society be formed of ingenious men residing in several colonies, to be called the American Philosophical Society." The core of this society lived in Philadelphia. The group met at least once a month and discussed the latest findings in botany, mathematics, chemistry, philosophy, and geology. The discussion was then sent to other members of the organization living in other cities and colonies. It brought together the bright-est minds in America, and Europe, and helped America gain in collective knowledge. Ben himself served as president of the society until his death. The American Philosophical Society still exists today.

An 1810 lithograph of the Pennsylvania Hospital, which Ben helped build

Before 1752, Philadelphia did not have a hospital. Instead, people who needed round-the-clock medical care were forced to hire a private nurse. Since most citizens could not afford this, they often went with little or no medical attention. But then Dr. Thomas Bond decided to start collecting contributions from the colony's wealthy citizens to build a hospital. He met with little success until he asked for help from the one person who could get the job done—Ben Franklin. "There is no such thing as carrying out a public-spirited project without you," Dr. Bond wrote in his letter to Ben. Ben threw himself into the task. He promoted the cause in his *Gazette,* held public meetings, and petitioned the Pennsylvania legislature for funds. His efforts succeeded. The hospital was founded in 1751 and admitted its first patient in 1752, and by 1755 construction was complete. Originally it contained only twenty beds and one doctor—Dr. Bond. But the hospital—which established a free drug dispensary and devoted itself to the humane treatment of the mentally ill—grew quickly. By Ben's death in 1790 two more bed-filled sections had been added and more doctors had been hired. The Pennsylvania Hospital still operates today.

BEN'S SCHOOL FOR BOYS

Ben wanted boys (his plans did not include girls) in Philadelphia to have the formal education he had lacked, so in 1749 he wrote a pamphlet called *Proposals Relating to the Education of Youth in Pennsylvania*. In it he argued that educational opportunities were missing in the colony, and proposed the building of a free school for boys between the ages of eight and sixteen. Ben's vision for this academy was crystal clear. It should be a house, he said, with a garden, orchard, and field. Its library should contain maps, globes, mathematical equipment for experiments, and prints. The teachers should set moral examples, be patient, and teach languages, science, the history of mankind, geography, oratory, proper reading, and writing techniques. Plenty of exercise, Ben stressed, was a must, and he hoped swimming would be taught. "It was," wrote Ben, "a grand scheme." But Ben did not stop there. After people had a chance to read *Proposals,* he began soliciting funds for building the school. Contributors to this building fund then chose twenty-four trustees to oversee the construction and eventual management of the school. Ben himself served as president of the board of trustees from 1749 to 1756. The Philadelphia Academy and Charitable School opened its doors in 1751 to any boy who showed intelligence and ability, regardless of financial means. The first of its kind in Pennsylvania, the school grew rapidly. Wrote Ben the following autumn, "We now have above one hundred students, and the number daily increasing." For the next thirty years the school continued to educate Pennsylvania's boys. Then in 1779, at the height of the American Revolution, the academy was accused of having pro-British sentiments. The state assembly (Pennsylvania's lawmaking body) seized control of the school. It tossed out the school's administrators, rechartered it as a school of higher learning, and renamed it the University of Pennsylvania, the name it still uses today.

A   W O M A N ' S   P L A C E

Ben was innovative, far thinking, a pioneer in many fields. But when it came to women, he was a man of his time.

In the 1700s American women had no rights and few opportunities. They could not vote or own property. They could not study in colleges or have careers. Instead they were expected to be "virtuous females," living their lives as dutiful daughters, diligent wives, and hardworking homemakers. Observed one Englishwoman who traveled to Philadelphia in 1785, "Nothing but insignificance and drudgery awaits a woman here."

Apparently Ben never considered the limitations placed on women. Instead, holding fast to the idea that a woman's place was in the home, he wrote this letter detailing his vision of the "ideal female":

> *With the best natural disposition in the world, she discovers daily the seeds and tokens of industry, economy, and in short, of every female virtue . . . and if success answers the married couple's fond wishes and expectations, she will, in the true sense of the word, be worth a great deal of money, and consequently, a great fortune.*

Women as cost-effective was a theme Ben returned to again and again. In his autobiography he claimed he had been "lucky" in finding a wife as "disposed to industry and frugality as myself," later admitting she "became a fortune to me." When his sister Jane married, he first thought to send her a "pretty little tea table for her parlor" but then considered that "the character of a good housewife is preferable to that of being a pretty gentlewoman." He sent her a spinning wheel instead.

Women who did not help make their husband's fortune were, in Ben's opinion, "useless." The very first edition of *Poor Richard's Almanack* included this jab at "idle females":

> *Many estates are spent in the getting*
> *When women for tea forsake spinning and knitting.*

Women had no place in Ben's educational ideas either. When his young friend Polly Stevenson talked of devoting herself to studying philosophy, Ben was appalled. "Knowledge may be useful," he warned her, "but there is nothing of equal dignity and importance than being a good daughter, a good wife, a good mother." Ben wondered why women needed the "full Pandora's box of knowledge" opened to them. Instead, he argued, women should be taught useful and functional skills—reading, writing, and accounting. This, he claimed, "stood them in good stead to be active, helpful partners in their husband's business."

Ben applied these beliefs to his own children. While William learned history, geometry, and philosophy, Sally learned to knit, spin, and embroider. Ben hired a Latin tutor for William; for Sally, he hired a tailor to teach her how to make buttonholes. And whereas Ben bragged that William was "a great lover of books," most of his references about Sally had to do with her domestic achievements, her sweet disposition, and her willingness to please. "Little Sally," Ben once wrote, "with her ready hands and feet, to do and go and come and get." It was, in short, a summation of his ideal woman—dutiful and virtuous.

Ben designed and printed this money for the Pennsylvania colony.

In the early 1700s colonists suffered from a constant shortage of money. The British would not allow Americans to mint their own coins, and they would not ship large exports of British silver coinage to the colonies. Also, the mother country demanded it be paid only in sterling. This sucked any hard money (coins of gold and silver) the colonists did have back across the Atlantic, making the shortage of money even worse. How could Americans buy and sell without money? Ben favored the idea of printing and circulating paper money, which he'd used while living in London in 1724. He believed paper money would be easier for colonists to handle. He also thought they would be more willing to spend it, which would boost business and trade, thus improving everyone's standard of living. "Money generates money," he wrote. Eventually the Pennsylvania Assembly agreed. In 1730 it passed a measure calling for the creation of paper money to be used and circulated among the colony's shopkeepers and tradesmen. And twenty-four-year-old Ben was given the job of printing it. Since counterfeiting was one of the biggest problems with paper money, Ben decided to create elaborately designed bills that would be hard to reproduce. To achieve this goal he built America's first copperplate press—a method of printing he'd seen in London. Duplicating what he had observed there, he engraved curlicues and intricate patterns of leaves in the soft copper plates. After a few in-between steps he inked the plates and pressed them to sturdy paper. The finished product pleased the assembly, and they extended his contract. Eventually New Jersey's assembly, impressed with Ben's work, asked him to print paper money for their colony as well. Even today Ben maintains a connection to paper money. His face is on the front of our one-hundred-dollar bill.

WEALTH FOR NO PURPOSE

Although he became very wealthy, Ben never spent money in any way he felt was not sensible. He lived by the motto "Waste not, want not" and believed one of the worst vices was "the pursuit of money for no purpose."

Ben liked to tell of the time a friend showed him through his new mansion. His friend took him into a living room big enough to house Congress. Why, asked Ben, would he want a room so big? "Because I can afford it," replied his friend. Next came a dining room large enough to seat fifty people. Again Ben wondered at the size, and again the friend said, "I can afford it." Ben at last turned to his friend. "Why are you wearing such a small hat? Why not get one ten times the size of your head? You can afford that, too!"

BEN BECOMES DEPUTY POSTMASTER GENERAL FOR AMERICA

In 1753 King George III gave Ben the job of overseeing the postal system in all thirteen colonies. Ben knew the snail-paced system badly needed improvement. When the mail wasn't lost or stolen, it took weeks for delivery—a month and a half for a letter to travel from Philadelphia to New York City. Immediately Ben set off on a journey to see for himself how things might be further improved. He spoke with postal riders, consulting with them on new, more direct routes. He insisted local postmasters keep accurate accounts and ordered them to print in the newspapers the names of persons who had letters waiting for them. People who did not want to pick up their mail at their post office had it delivered for the price of a penny, the beginning of home delivery. Ben also had all unclaimed letters forwarded to Philadelphia, creating the very first dead-letter office. These changes, and others, completely overhauled the postal system. By Ben's fourth year the postal service turned a profit for the first time, and with the introduction of night travel for postal riders, a Philadelphia writer could post a letter for New York one day and receive a reply back the next! But more important, this new, improved mail service pulled the distant regions of the colonies together. It began cementing the scattered colonies into one unified country—America.

FRANKLIN'S POST-RIDER.

Traveling by His Wits

Traveling was a rugged business in the 1750s, and only someone with Ben's toughness could have endured bad weather, rutted roads, quagmires of mud, and suffocating dust. Taverns and inns were few and overcrowded. To get a spot by the fire after many grueling hours in the saddle was almost impossible—impossible, that is, unless you were Ben Franklin.

On a raw, rainy day Deputy Postmaster General Franklin stopped at a Rhode Island tavern only to find two dozen travelers crowded around the room's only fire.

"Boy!" Ben called to the tavern keeper's son. "Get my horse a quart of oysters."

"A quart of oysters?" gasped the boy.

"You heard me, a quart of oysters," boomed Ben.

The boy obeyed, followed by two dozen men who hurried from the fire to see this incredible sight—a horse who ate oysters!

Minutes later the baffled boy and men returned to the tavern. "Sir," said the boy, "your horse won't eat the oysters."

"No?" replied Ben from his cozy chair beside the fire. "Then bring me the oysters, and take some hay to my horse."

A FAR-SIGHTED PLAN

As postmaster, Ben traveled across the thirteen colonies, providing him with a unique perspective. He didn't see thirteen separate territories. He saw one country—America. And he saw it long before anyone else.

America! It was a bold idea for the mid-eighteenth century. At that time colonists considered themselves Pennsylvanians, New Yorkers, Virginians, or Massachusetts men. Their laws came from England, and they pledged their loyalty to King George III.

But Ben thought differently. He thought the colonies should unite. "All we want is order and discipline," he argued. "*Union* will make us strong."

His ideas, however, might have gone unheard if England and France had not begun fighting in 1754. (War was not officially declared until 1756.) Called the French and Indian War by the colonists because the French and Native Americans were allied against the British and the colonists, it was to decide who was to rule in North America. Suddenly, a plan for a common intercolonial defense was urgently needed. In 1754 each colony sent representatives to Albany, New York, to hash out a plan. Ben was chosen as Pennsylvania's representative, and he seized the opportunity to promote his idea of uniting the colonies. Quickly, he sketched out a workable plan. Called the Albany Plan of Union, it created a governor general and a grand council consisting of members chosen by each colony's assembly. This united government would have the power to raise taxes for defense of the American colonies. It would be allowed to form militia and build forts and stockades. Colonists would make their own decisions, but the British government in London would approve them. Pleased with his work, Ben went off to Albany, confident the others would approve it.

He was wrong. "I thought you a wise man," scolded one Massachusetts representative, "but you . . . have shown yourself by your projected plan for an Union to be an arrant blockhead. . . . The world can see through your scheme in a minute." Colony after colony rejected the plan. Even Pennsylvania refused to sign it. Why? Colonists believed it took away too much of their local control, while London thought it came too close to creating a political body strong enough to challenge Parliament.

Ben was bitterly disappointed. "Everyone cries, a union is absolutely necessary; but when they come to the manner and form of the union, their weak noodles are distracted."

Eventually he came to feel that if the Albany Plan had been signed, the Revolutionary War would have been avoided. "I am still of the opinion that it would have been happy for both sides of the water if the plan had been adopted. The colonies so united would have been sufficiently strong to have defended themselves; there would have been no need of troops from England, of course the subsequent taxing of America and the bloody contest it occasioned would never have occurred. But such mistakes are not new; history is full of errors."

Ben was right. After the French and Indian War, thousands of British troops remained in the colonies. Their job was to patrol the wilderness frontiers, and protect British subjects. This army, however, was expensive to maintain. Eventually King George and his advisors decided American colonists should pay the cost through taxes on items such as stamps and tea. It was the beginning of big trouble.

As James Madison, father of the Constitution and fourth president of the United States, later said, Ben had summed up the whole argument of the American Revolution "within the compass of a nutshell twenty years before it occurred to anyone else."

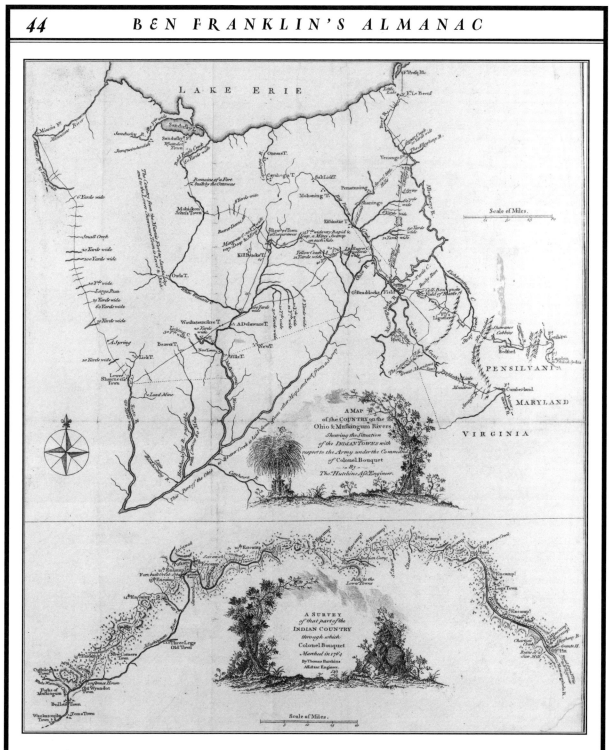

A map of what Ben called the "Middle English Colonies"

Because of the fast-growing population in the colonies Ben firmly believed America's future lay to the west. He was one of the first people to look beyond the Appalachian Mountains. And what did he see? "Vast, unsettled lands ripe for development of farms and cities." He saw Americans consuming more, producing more, growing prosperous. And he saw himself as governor of this territory. He even petitioned King George III to grant him the charters for two colonies on land that is now Ohio and Indiana, but the Revolution interrupted his attempts. Still, his enthusiasm for the West did not go unappreciated. The first territory west of the Appalachian Mountains was called Franklin until it was renamed Tennessee.

GENERAL BEN FRANKLIN DIRECTS THE BUILDING OF A STOCKADE FORT

On November 24, 1755, a group of Shawnee attacked a village on Pennsylvania's frontier. In response the colony's governor conferred on Ben the military rank of general and in January 1756 sent him west to supervise the construction of a fort. Ben had never built a fort before. But he had read a book called *A Short Treatise on Fortification and Geometry.* The book helped. Despite rainy weather, rough quarters, and bad food, fifty-year-old General Franklin and his five hundred men built the fort in just six days. Then he happily turned his command over to one of the soldiers and went home. His military career had lasted less than a month.

"The March of the Paxton Men," a cartoon from 1764 showing Ben (right) cheering his supporters

ON DECEMBER 14, 1763, a gang of Scotch-Irish settlers known as the Paxton Men attacked a village of peaceful Native Americans living on Pennsylvania's frontiers. The entire village—made up mostly of women, children, and the elderly—was wiped out. This attack outraged Ben. He lashed out by writing:

> *All good people everywhere detest your actions. Cowards! [He underlined the word twice.] The only crime of these people seems to have been that they had a reddish brown skin, and black hair. If it be right to kill men for such reasons, then why should we not kill people with white skin, or red hair? In short, it appears they would have been safe in any part of the world except in the neighborhood of the white, Christian savage!*

Infuriated by Ben's words, the settlers marched on Philadelphia. As one thousand rioters approached the city its citizens panicked. Luckily Ben kept his head and hastily gathered together members of the Philadelphia militia. With Ben in the lead, the troop rode out to meet the rebels. "The fighting face we put on, the reasoning we used with the insurgents . . . turned them back and restored quiet to the city." Ben's bravery and levelheadedness was noted by Philadelphians. Ever after Ben Franklin would be the man to turn to when problems needed solutions.

Looking to the Future

Ben's strong interest and influence in Pennsylvania never waned. But while he continued to improve city streets, provide for defense, and form human services, a new, intense interest grabbed his attention.

I should like to give myself leisure to read, study, make experiments.

THE SCIENTIST'S SCRAPBOOK

As we enjoy great advantages from the invention of others, we should be glad of an opportunity to serve others by any invention of ours. —Benjamin Franklin, *AUTOBIOGRAPHY*, 1771

Ben's first experiment

ONE MORNING while flying a kite, nine-year-old Ben came to a pond. Deciding to go for a swim, he shed his clothes, tied his kite to a tree branch, and dived in. He floated awhile before noticing the kite still soaring in the air. His mind clicked, and he was struck with an idea—the idea of combining his two favorite activities. "I found that lying on my back and holding the stick in my hands, I was drawn along the surface of the water in a very agreeable manner. Having then engaged another boy to carry my clothes . . . to a place . . . on the other side, I began to cross the pond with my kite, which carried me quite over without the least fatigue and with the greatest pleasure imaginable." Describing this event many years later to a fellow scientist in France, Ben speculated that it might be possible to cross the English Channel the same way. But on second thought he concluded, "A boat would be more comfortable."

A "magic square of squares" composed by Ben

As a boy, Ben became obsessed with creating "magic squares of squares," a mathematical stunt of numbering squares so that the sums of every row— horizontal, diagonal, vertical—are equal. Simple at first, his squares grew more complicated as his math skills grew. By the time Ben reached adulthood, making magic squares had become a favorite pastime—particularly during those dragging sessions of the Pennsylvania Assembly. Bored, he worked out these mathematical puzzles while his fellow assemblymen prattled on about trivial matters. When his scientist friends later discovered this, they asked him to publish the most difficult one he had ever created. Ben did.
"You will readily admit," he wrote in an accompanying letter,
"that this square of 16 is the most magically magical of any magic square ever made by any magician."

200	217	232	249	8	25	40	57	72	89	104	121	136	153	168	181
58	39	26	7	250	231	218	199	186	167	154	135	122	103	90	71
198	219	230	251	6	27	38	59	70	91	102	123	134	155	166	187
60	37	28	5	252	229	220	197	188	165	156	133	124	101	92	69
201	216	233	248	9	24	41	56	73	88	105	120	137	152	169	184
55	42	23	10	247	234	215	202	183	170	151	138	119	106	87	74
203	214	235	246	11	22	43	54	75	86	107	118	139	150	171	182
53	44	21	12	245	236	213	204	181	172	149	140	117	108	85	76
205	212	237	244	13	20	45	52	77	84	109	116	141	148	173	180
51	46	19	14	243	238	211	206	179	174	147	142	115	110	83	78
207	210	239	242	15	18	47	50	79	82	111	114	143	146	175	178
49	48	17	16	241	240	209	208	177	176	145	144	113	112	81	80
196	221	228	253	4	29	36	61	68	93	100	125	132	157	164	189
62	35	30	3	254	227	222	195	190	163	158	131	126	99	94	67
194	223	226	255	2	31	34	63	66	95	98	127	130	159	162	191
64	33	32	1	256	225	224	193	192	161	160	129	128	97	96	65

AN EIGHTEENTH-CENTURY ENGRAVING SHOWS HOW TO MAKE BEN FRANKLIN'S STOVE

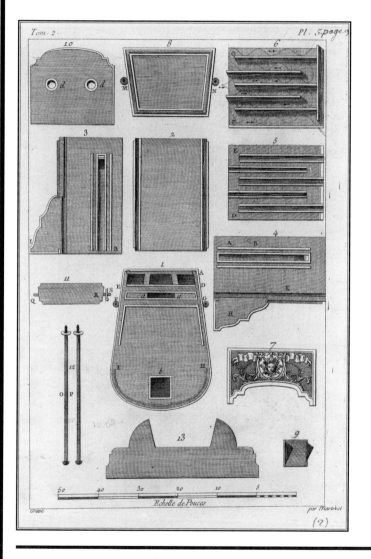

Ben gave much thought to Philadelphia's cold winters. Many times he sat before his fireplace, burning his knees while his back end froze, and wondered if he could improve heating systems. In 1741 he did. Calling his new invention the "Pennsylvania Fireplace," Ben claimed it "gave out twice as much heat, but used only a fourth as much wood." Made of nine iron plates, the stove directed heat into the room and smoke up the chimney—instead of the other way around. Ben put one in his own home and published a pamphlet with detailed instructions and illustrations so others could learn about it. Said Ben, the stove was "so completely described that any good blacksmith can make one." His invention quickly grew popular in the colonies, and people began calling it the Franklin stove in tribute to the man who warmed their homes. Wood-burning stoves based on Ben's design are still used today.

THE WAYS OF ANTS

Ben's boundless curiosity led him to explore, examine, and observe everything around him. Even the tiniest creatures did not escape his notice.

Wondering why ants always found their way into his molasses jar, even after he moved it, Ben tried an experiment. He shook out all but one of the little insects from the jar, then hung the jar by a string from a nail in the ceiling. Ben watched the remaining ant eat its fill, then find its way up the string to the ceiling and down the wall to the floor. Half an hour later a swarm of ants arrived as if, wrote Ben, "they had been told the news, followed the course the pioneer ant had taken, ate till they finished, then left by string and ceiling." From this experiment Ben deduced that "ants have a language all their own."

Ben's sketch of the electrical apparatus used in his experiments

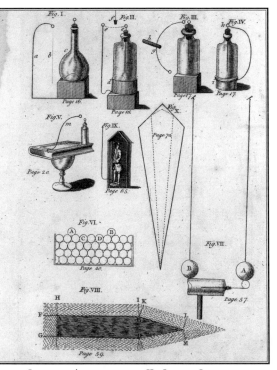

When Ben began his studies, electricity was more curiosity than science. Showmen called electricians traveled the colonies giving "shocks to the public," as a form of entertainment. One of the most common demonstrations involved suspending a boy from the ceiling with numerous silken cords and rubbing his bare feet with glass tubes that drew "electrical fire"—that is, sparks—from his face and hands. In 1743 an electrician named "Dr. Spence" performed this very trick in Boston. Thirty-seven-year-old Ben, who was in town on postal business, was so delighted and intrigued by the performance, he bought Spence's devices—tubes, wires, and all. Already understanding that metal conducts electricity, he added a pewter saltshaker, an iron pump handle, and five brass thimbles taken from his wife's sewing basket. Later he added tin bells, brass balls, and a Leyden jar—a glass tube, coated inside and outside with metal foil, that can hold a single electric charge. Arranging all this in his upstairs study, Ben now had what he called his "electrical laboratory." And he soon had plenty of time to do experiments there. In 1748 he retired from the active business of printing, handing over the day-to-day operation to friend and partner David Hall.

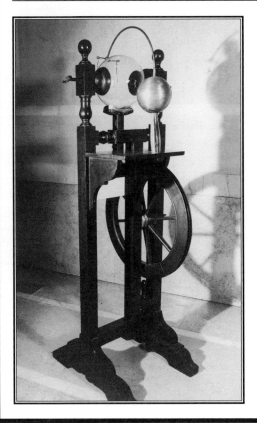

BEN BUILT THIS EARLY ELECTRICAL GENERATOR FOR HIS EXPERIMENTS

Ben had one big problem when he first began his electrical experiments—supplying himself with enough of the elusive element. He would need more than a spark or two. Knowing that two items when rubbed together can "make a friction that can create electrical fire," Ben enlarged on this principle. He invented what he called his "electrostatic machine." By revolving the glass globe against a piece of chamois skin, a charge of static electricity was built in the globe. The charge was drawn off by a set of knitting needles and stored in a Leyden jar. Ben's problem was solved. The electrostatic machine provided an easy and endless supply of electricity for his experiments. It also laid the groundwork for the invention of the modern-day generator.

FUN WITH ELECTRICITY

Ben was a serious scientist, but not all the time. Many of his experiments were designed to draw laughter as well as lightning.

Almost as soon as Ben began his experiments in 1745, people flocked to observe them. "My house," he wrote, "was continually full . . . with persons who came to see these new wonders." Ben did not disappoint them, producing bolts of lightning, causing brass balls to glow red, and making his ring of gray hair stand on end.

One of his favorite experiments was called "The Counterfeit Spider." Using a burned cork for the body and linen thread for the legs, Ben attached his "spider" to a wire. When the wire was electrified by touching it to an electrical battery or Leyden jar, the spider jumped, wiggled, and ran across Ben's worktable, startling the spectators. Noted Ben with a wink, "The little spider appeared perfectly alive to anyone unacquainted with the trick."

Another experiment that made visitors laugh was "The Golden Fish." Ben electrified a piece of gold leaf shaped like a fish, causing it to wiggle, shake its tail, and "swim" across the table. The fish stopped at Ben's finger, where it appeared to nibble it.

Ben once invited a group of friends to an "electrical picnic." He planned to kill a turkey by "electrical shock," then roast it with "electrical fire." Unfortunately, he became so engrossed in conversation he forgot to pay close attention to what he was doing. He touched two wires together and *zap*! Ben received the shock instead of the turkey. His body vibrated from head to toe, and smoke curled from one buckled shoe. Luckily he escaped with just a few bruises and a sore chest.

Even though he enjoyed an audience, there were days when Ben longed to work uninterrupted. At those times he scattered the gawkers gathered in front of his house by sending a snapping, sizzling surge of electricity through his wrought-iron fence. The responding squeals and screams gave Ben more than a few private laughs.

"Let the experiment be made!" Ben always said. When it came to electricity, he made some fun ones.

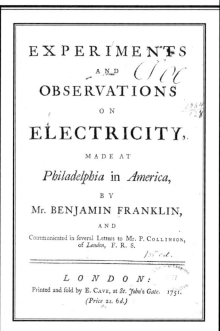

TITLE PAGE FROM THE BOOK THAT MADE BEN A WORLD-FAMOUS SCIENTIST

Ben discovered the properties of electricity through careful experimentation and observation. Step by step, he set down his progress in a series of letters addressed to his friend and fellow scientist Peter Collinson. Collinson, who lived in London, believed Ben's work should be shared with others. He gathered Ben's letters together and in 1751 published them in this eighty-six-page book, *Experiments and Observations of Electricity.* Immediately the book was translated into French, German, Italian, and Latin as scientists from England to Russia grappled with its theories and replicated its experiments.

It made Ben a household name among scientists even before he'd performed his historic experiment with kite and key.

Ben and his son, William, wait for lightning to strike.

On a June afternoon in 1752 a storm was brewing, a bad one, with thunder and dangerous lightning. Only one man in Philadelphia greeted this storm with delight—Ben Franklin. Convinced that electricity and lightning were the same thing, Ben had decided to fly a kite into "the very heart of the storm," to test his theory. His kite was odd looking. Made of silk because it was "fitter to bear the wet and wind of a thunder gust" than paper, the kite had a miniature metal rod poking from its top to conduct electricity. This rod, Ben explained, would "draw fire from the clouds." A hemp twine ran from the kite to the ground. Dry hemp conducted electricity reasonably well, but wet hemp "conducted the electricity fire freely." Near the bottom of the twine a brass key was tied. This would absorb any electric charge that ran down the string. And in case the kite flyer received a jolt, a silk handkerchief was attached to the end of the twine. It would help insulate the flyer's hand from twine and key. With this unusual kite in tow, father and son raced to a nearby open field. As Ben took shelter in the shepherd's shed William raced three times across the rain-lashed pasture. Finally the kite took flight, and William hurried into the shed, where he handed the string to Ben. Ben tried to avoid the forks of lightning streaking across the sky—he knew it was too dangerous to fly his kite directly into those. Instead he flew it into the thunderclouds, hoping he would be able to detect the presence of electricity. Moments later a "very promising cloud" passed overhead. Ben touched his knuckle to the key. Nothing. Could it be his hypothesis was wrong? Were electricity and lightning two different things? Then Ben noticed something unusual. The loose threads on the kite were standing straight up. Excitedly, Ben touched the key again. He felt the familiar tingling of electric shock. It was true! Electricity and lightning were one and the same. Ben was overcome with wonder. But for the man who talked about almost everything, he said very little about this event. He did not even record the exact day or time his experiment took place and kept the discovery a secret for several months before finally reporting it to the scientific world.

E L E C T R I C I T Y   1 0 1

Although many of Ben's electrical discoveries seem basic nowadays, they were stunning and groundbreaking in the mid-1700s. These are some of his discoveries:

1. An electric charge can be stored. Improving on the Leyden jar, which had recently been invented at the University of Leyden in Holland, Ben designed a glass jar with tinfoil coatings inside and outside. A brass rod touching the inner foil transferred an electric charge from its original source (usually Ben's electrostatic machine) to the jar. The charge was then stored until the brass rod was connected to a conductor (see below). A rubber stopper prevented the brass rod from touching the neck of the jar, which could cause the electric charge to leak away.

Leyden jar

2. Ben expanded on the Leyden jar to create an early electrical battery. Using a glass and lead arrangement (of which, sadly, few details exist), he was able to produce electricity by a reaction between two different metals. Although Ben's battery did not produce the steady flow of electricity modern-day batteries do, it did produce several sparks, a vast improvement over the Leyden jar's single surge.

3. An electric charge can move through some materials better than others. Ben called these materials conductors and determined that metals, as well as water, made the best conductors.

4. Some materials, such as wood, silk, and glass, resist the movement of an electric charge. Ben called these materials insulators.

5. Ben also coined the terms "positive" and "negative" to describe the amount of electricity in/on an object.

6. The flow of an electric charge can be a direct current, flowing steadily in one direction, or an alternating current, flowing back and forth and changing direction.

7. Both lightning and an electric charge give off light, are swift in motion, make a noise when exploding, can exist in water or ice, can tear objects they pass through, can kill, can melt metals, can cause fire, and sometimes make a sulfurous smell.

B E N   B E C O M E S   A   D O C T O R

For his electrical achievements Ben received many honors. The Royal Society, the elite of the English scientific world, elected him a member and bestowed upon him its greatest honor, the Copley Medal. The king of France sent personal congratulations. And Harvard, Yale, and Oxford Universities gave him honorary degrees. These last honors especially delighted Ben, who had only two years of formal education. Ever after he insisted people address him using his new title—Dr. Franklin. He described his feelings in a letter to a New England friend:

> I feel like the young girl who was observed to grow suddenly proud, and none could guess the reason till it came to be known that she had got on a pair of new, silk garters. . . . Though I do not hide my honors under a petticoat . . . I fear I have not so much reason to be proud as the girl had; for a feather in one's cap is not so useful a thing, or so serviceable to the wearer, than a pair of good silk garters.

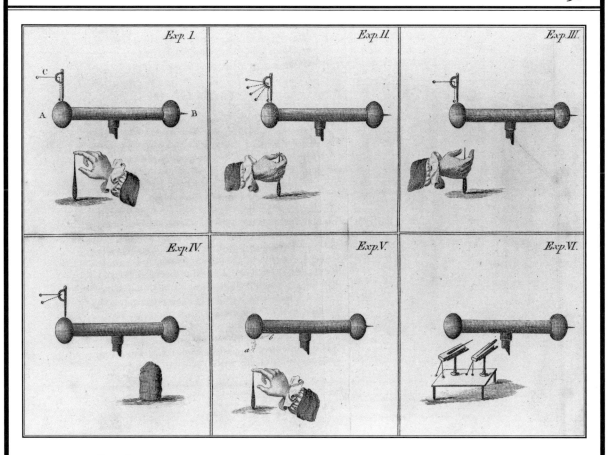

BEN'S DRAWING OF HIS BUILDING-SAVING LIGHTNING ROD

Ben's discovery that lightning is electricity led directly to his invention of the lightning rod. He advised, "One should fix at the highest parts [of buildings] rods of iron made sharp as a needle . . . and from the foot of these needles a wire down the outside of the building into the ground thus drawing the electricity away from the building and protecting them from lightning." Ben mounted a rod on his own roof in September 1753. In October he described his invention in detail in *Poor Richard's Almanack* so everyone could benefit. But not everyone embraced his invention. Many believed a home destroyed by lightning was God's will, and it was sacrilegious to erect a rod. Others argued the rod really attracted lightning, or worse, collected it in the center of the earth until it caused an earthquake. Still, cities around the world gradually sprouted these small, sharp spires from their roofs, sparing thousands of buildings from fire and destruction.

BEN FRANKLIN, WIZARD OF ELECTRICITY

In the eighteenth century people considered scientists to be a bit like sorcerers. Ben, who had tamed lightning and delved into the mysteries of electricity, gained a magical, almost superhuman image. People whispered about him, repeated tales of his divine powers, and declared him a true wizard. Ben found this reputation annoying. "Being witness to something extraordinary [man] is ready to believe the wildest absurdities—such is the logic of three-fourths of the human race," he once said. But while Ben tried to avoid his mystic reputation, Mason Chamberlin, the artist who painted this portrait in 1762, did not. Chamberlin included not only the bells Ben had rigged up in his laboratory, but an electrical storm raging outside as well. "It hints of mystical powers," Ben once said of the portrait. It was never one of his favorites.

Ben's drawing of the glass armonica, a musical instrument he invented

Ben loved music and played several instruments, including the violin, harp, and guitar. In 1761 he decided to try his hand at inventing a musical instrument. Called the glass armonica, it consisted of a row of thirty-seven open-necked glass jars of varying sizes. These glasses were arranged, largest to smallest, on an iron spindle that turned when the player pumped a foot treadle. The player then touched the whirling glasses with fingers that were "thoroughly wet." Ben claimed the music made by the armonica was "heavenly . . . ethereal . . . incomparably sweet." Others thought so too. For the next three decades the armonica was the musical rage. In London copies of the instrument sold wildly. In Paris, Queen Marie Antoinette demanded armonica lessons. And in Austria and Germany noted composers Mozart and Beethoven wrote music for it. But the armonica craze did not last long. By 1800 the instrument had grown obsolete. Eventually it was forgotten.

BEN'S CHART SHOWS THE COURSE OF THE GULF STREAM

On his trips across the Atlantic Ocean, Ben noticed a path of water that was a different color from the rest of the sea, and he decided to study it. He noted that no whales swam in it. He also noted that more weeds grew in it and that it did not sparkle in the moonlight. By lowering a thermometer from the ship's deck, he learned it was a warmer temperature than the surrounding water. And by tossing objects into it, he determined its course. He concluded this path of water was really a river that flowed from Florida northeastward through the Atlantic Ocean. He also noticed it had an impact on the speed with which ships traveled between the American colonies and England. Trips toward England were faster because ships traveled with the stream, whereas trips toward the colonies were slower, as ships struggled against it. A map of this stream, Ben decided, would be extremely useful to sea captains. Using his observations, as well as information gleaned from sailors, Ben was able to draw an accurate chart, enabling ships to take advantage of the swifter current.

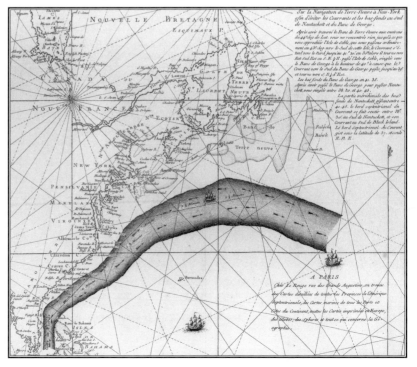

BEN'S DRAWING OF THE MASTODON BONES HE STUDIED

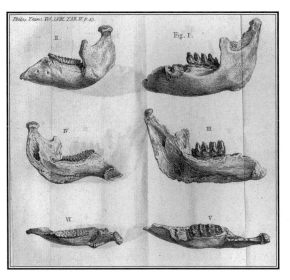

Because of his reputation other scientists often asked Ben for advice and opinions. One was George Croghan, who found several unusual fossils on a trip to Big Bone Lick, in Kentucky, in 1766. Puzzled by this find, he sent a portion of his collection to Ben, including "four great tusks, a joint of the vertebrae bone, and three large, pronged teeth." What did Ben make of these specimens? "Surely," Ben surmised, "such bones belong to some animal unknown, perhaps one which died away long ago. . . . It is puzzling to conceive why it perished . . . perhaps the climates were differently placed from what they are at present." Amazingly, Ben had hinted at theories that scientists would not explore for another one hundred years.

Ben writes to friend Polly Stevenson in his newly developed phonetic alphabet, July 20, 1768

Ben toyed with the idea of simplifying the English alphabet after noticing how badly many women spelled. Since most women received little formal education, they spelled by ear, writing words the way they sounded. Instead of criticizing them, Ben devised a new alphabet. He eliminated letters that did not match their sounds, such as q, x, and y, and created new letters he thought were needed. He then began writing to friends in his "improved alphabet." But he found few people ready to give up their familiar written language. As Ben himself later admitted, even he could not "uz a simplr verzun al hiz lyf."

BEN'S BIFOCALS

As an adult, Ben always wore glasses. Without them, he wrote, he could not "distinguish a letter even of large print." Still, he thought ordinary glasses impractical. Sometimes he needed help seeing close objects, and other times he had trouble focusing on things farther away. He carried around two pairs of glasses but found constant changing "troublesome." So in 1784 Ben asked a glass cutter to cut both pairs of lenses in half. Then he glued the bottoms of one set of lenses to the tops of the other. Now through the top half he could see far distances, while the bottom helped him see closer objects. "This I find most convenient," declared Ben.

AN EIGHTEENTH-CENTURY ENGRAVING OF THE GERMAN VERSION OF THE FRESH-AIR BATH, ANOTHER INNOVATION OF BEN'S

Ben had very definite ideas about maintaining good health. He believed in regular exercise, frequent tub bathing, and a diet full of fruits and vegetables—radical ideas in the 1700s. Even more radical, he believed in the healthful benefits of cold, fresh air when most people thought cold air was bad for one's lungs. "I have found it more agreeable to my constitution to bathe in another element. I mean cold air. . . . With this view I rise every morning, and sit in my chamber without any clothes whatsoever, half an hour, or an hour, depending on the season. This practice is not in the least painful, but, on the contrary, agreeable." Europeans, especially, expanded on his idea, building small "open air bathing houses" like the one shown.

DR. FRANKLIN'S LABORATORY

In 1787 a Massachusetts clergyman named Manasseh Cutler visited Philadelphia. More than anything, he wanted to meet Ben. He got his wish. Since Cutler was a member of the American Philosophical Society, Ben talked to him about scientific experiments and inventions, and even showed him his laboratory. Cutler described it this way.

> *The Doctor showed me a snake with two heads preserved in a large vial . . . and worked for me an invention for putting books, of which there were many, on high shelves. . . . Most impressive was the apparatus for making electricity, . . . a glass machine exhibiting the circulation of blood into the arteries and veins, . . . and a rolling press he invented for copying letters.*

But Cutler was most taken with Ben's "great armed chair with rockers, and a large fan over it, with which he fans himself, keeps off the flies, etc., while he sits reading with only a small motion of his foot."

A GRAB BAG OF INVENTIONS, OBSERVATIONS, AND EXPERIMENTS

One day while out for a walk, Ben noticed a woven basket imported from Europe lying in the streambed. The reeds from which the basket was made had sprouted in the water, and tiny leaves were unfolding. "That basket is alive!" Ben declared. He took a couple of the sprouted reeds home and planted them in his backyard. It was the beginning of willow trees in America.

Ben experimented with the effects of heat on cloth of different colors. One winter he cut out four squares of fabric—black, dark blue, light blue, and white. He arranged them on top of a backyard snowdrift in the direct rays of the sun. The black cloth quickly melted into the snow. The dark blue cloth was only slightly less buried. The light blue cloth melted into the snow a little bit. But at the end of the experiment the white cloth still lay on top of the snow. This convinced Ben that "light-colored clothing should be worn in hot weather, as light colors resist heat."

Ben frequently suffered from the common cold and desperately wanted to discover its cause and cure. He observed that being subjected to damp or cold weather rarely resulted in illness. "I have long been satisfied from observation that people often catch cold from one another when shut up together in closed rooms and carriages . . . when sitting near and conversing so as to breathe in each other's transpiration." He endorsed fresh air and clean hands. And since he also believed disease was caught from old clothes, old books, and decayed animal matter, he advocated clean surroundings. Without ever having heard the word *germs,* Ben discovered much of what we know about disease today.

Ben noted that people who worked with certain metals—potters, painters, glass-blowers, and printmakers—often grew ill with the same symptoms. Ben investigated and found that all used a common material—lead. He decided lead was poisonous and cautioned people not to use it. It was the first diagnosis of lead poisoning in history.

When still a boy, Ben loved to swim, but he always wished he could swim faster. He did some experimenting and found he could increase his speed through the water by attaching oval palettes to his hands. Later he invented something like flippers to attach to his feet, adding even more to his speed.

Ben invented shock treatment therapy when a woman who suffered "convulsive fits and hysterical symptoms" came to him for help. He gave her a series of electrical charges over the course of two weeks, then gave her a Leyden jar to take home and instructed her to electrify herself with it every day for three weeks. "The symptoms gradually decreased till at length they entirely left me," she reported. Electroshock therapy is still used in the treatment of mental illness today.

A Scientist to the End

In his eighty-fourth year Ben's illness and old age kept him confined to bed. Despite his physical limitations, his mind was as sharp as ever. From his bedroom he pondered and hypothesized. And he conducted one last experiment for an old friend who wrote to him complaining of deafness.

"Your problem might be solved by putting your thumb behind your ear, pressing it outwards and enlarging it, as it were, with the hollow of your hand," Ben told his friend. This was not an old wives' tale. It actually worked, as Ben proved. "By an exact experiment I found that I could hear the tick of a watch at forty-five feet distance by this means, which was barely audible at twenty-five without it."

REVOLUTIONARY MEMORABILIA

Those who give up essential liberty to preserve a little temporary safety, deserve neither liberty, nor safety.

—BENJAMIN FRANKLIN, 1759

The War Before

The dispute between England and the American colonies had been simmering since the French and Indian War began in 1756. France and England, each with their Native American allies, had fought for years over who would rule North America. The largest group of Native Americans known as the Iroquois of New York—a confederacy of six Indian nations—sided with England, while most of the other native tribes sided with France. After seven years of fighting, England emerged victorious. France's holdings in North America were greatly reduced.

But England's problems were far from over. The war had left that country with a huge debt. The government needed money to pay that debt, as well as to support the thousands of British soldiers who would now be required to patrol America's wilderness frontier. Where could money be found? King George III and his advisers turned to America. The colonists, they declared, should pay for the cost of the war through taxes.

Americans disagreed. They had fought as faithful British subjects in the war. They had given money, too, piling up their own war debt. Besides, they didn't want all those British troops living in their midst. They had their own militias—that is, volunteer armies—and while these militias were not well armed, or well trained, they felt perfectly capable of defending themselves. More important, they insisted they should not be taxed at all by Parliament. It was their right, colonists argued, to vote on their own taxes in their own assemblies, as they'd been doing all along.

A personal favorite of Ben's and his family's, this portrait shows him as colonial agent and politician during his years in England.

I N 1756 members of Pennsylvania's legislature —called the Pennsylvania Assembly—began arguing with the king's representatives over a proposed property tax that would pay for colonial defense. The king's representatives insisted their vast estates be exempted from the tax, while assembly members insisted they be included. The argument between the two parties became so heated that finally the assembly appointed Ben as their agent and sent him to London to take up the matter directly with the king. Ben arrived in England in 1757 ready to iron out the differences. But a greater American problem soon overshadowed this minor one: Could the British government tax the American colonies, which were not represented in Parliament? England and the colonies quarreled over the answer for the next nineteen years. Ben, who remained in England almost the entire time (he returned home from 1762 to 1764), wrote articles, organized petitions, attended meetings, and tried desperately to reconcile "the mother country with her child."

NUMBER 7 CRAVEN STREET, BEN'S HOME IN LONDON

In 1757 Ben arrived in London with his twenty-seven-year-old son, William, and quickly rented an apartment in one of the most fashionable areas in the city. "We have four rooms furnished," Ben wrote to Deborah, "and everything about us pretty genteel." Besides finding fine living quarters, Ben made lifelong friends on Craven Street. Margaret Stevenson, the charming widow who owned the house, doted on Ben. She did his shopping, fixed his favorite foods, and nursed him through his illnesses. Her daughter, Polly, was intelligent, sensible, and good natured. Ben loved her as a daughter from the first. When he left the Stevenson home after sixteen years, all felt heartbroken. Eventually devoted Polly moved to Philadelphia to be close to her "dear Papa."

King George III, the man Ben grew to hate

Some of the harshest words found in Ben's writings are against England's monarch, George III. But Ben hadn't always raged against the king. Ben happily attended George's coronation in 1760. Afterward he wrote, "I am of the opinion that his virtue and . . . sincere intentions to make his people happy will give him steadiness." But Ben soon came to believe that George did not care about the happiness of his people—especially those living in the American colonies. Meanwhile, the king grew more resentful of the belligerence and rebellion he thought he saw in Americans. He advocated using severe restrictions and force to make the colonists bend to his will. "I refuse," he declared, "to ever compromise!" By 1776 Ben no longer wanted to compromise either. "This king," Ben raged, "will stand foremost in the list of diabolical, bloody and execrable tyrants!"

A STAMP MANUFACTURED FOR THE STAMP ACT

In 1765 the debt-ridden British government passed the Stamp Act as a means of raising money. The act required colonists who produced certain printed materials to buy British tax stamps to paste on them—a stamp for each page of a newspaper or pamphlet, for every will, legal contract, marriage license, diploma, even playing cards, calendars, advertisements, and dice. Worse, the act specified payment for these stamps be made in "hard money," that is, only in gold or silver coin. Since most colonies now used paper currency, hard money was often impossible to find. And if colonists chose not to buy stamps? The act declared that violators would be tried in an admiralty court, which meant there would be no jury. "This act," declared Ben, "is the mother of mischief." "This act," cried the colonists, "is taxation without representation." Without a voice in Parliament, colonists firmly believed, taxes could not be imposed on them.

A MOB OF ANGRY COLONISTS SURROUNDS BEN'S PHILADELPHIA HOME AFTER PARLIAMENT PASSES THE STAMP ACT

In response to the Stamp Act resentful colonists took to the streets, burning, looting, and in a few cases, tarring and feathering government officials. In Philadelphia a false rumor spread that the Franklins favored the Stamp Act. A mob quickly gathered in front of their house. Although he was in London, Ben heard the news from wife Deborah in this vivid, if badly spelled, letter: "I feched a gun or two. . . . We maid one room into a magazin. I ordored sum sorte of defen upstairs such as I could manaig my self." When neighbors told her to flee, she refused. "I sed . . . I was verey shur you had dun nothing to hurte aney bodey." The mob eventually dispersed.

This news deeply disturbed Ben. He was stunned by the temper of his countrymen and upset by their violence. He realized the Stamp Act would have to be repealed . . . or else.

BEN IS QUESTIONED BY PARLIAMENT ABOUT THE COLONIES' FEELINGS TOWARD THE STAMP ACT.

British lawmakers were surprised by America's fury over the Stamp Act. Wanting to understand how this had happened, in 1766 they invited a series of expert witnesses to testify before them. One was Ben Franklin. Always the shrewd politician, Ben decided to make sure his testimony had real impact. So he wrote several questions in advance. He rehearsed the answers to the questions. Then he passed along his questions to a friend, who happened to be a member of Parliament. On the day Ben gave testimony, that friend asked the prearranged questions:

Q: *Do you think the people of America would submit to pay the stamp duty if it was moderated (limited or changed)?*
Ben: *No, never, unless compelled by force of arms. . . .*
Q: *What was the temper of Americans toward Great Britain before the year 1763?*
Ben: *The best in the world. They submitted willingly to the government of the Crown. . . . They had not only a respect, but an affection for Great Britain, for its laws, its customs and manners, and even a fondness for its fashions. . . .*
Q: *And what is their temper now?*
Ben: *Oh, very much altered.*

As Ben spoke, Parliament members were, as one witness wrote, "all ears." Some may even have noticed Ben's choice of words. Using "its" and "theirs," he implied the colonies' new, and growing, sense of separation from England.

THE STAMP ACT IS BURIED,
AS SHOWN IN THIS EIGHTEENTH-CENTURY CARTOON.

One week after he appeared before Parliament, Ben ecstatically wrote, "I am just now made very happy by a vote . . . for the repeal of the Stamp Act." And colonists were made happy too. His testimony had directly brought this about. When the news was published in America, people throughout the colonies cheered him, drinking toasts to his "genius and brave spirit." People in England, however, were less thrilled. British newspapers published cartoons like this one, depicting Parliament's prime minister burying his brainchild of a tax in a family vault where other repealed laws had been interred. Still, most people on both sides of the Atlantic believed trouble had been avoided—but not Ben. Even though Parliament had repealed the act, it still maintained the right to tax the colonies whenever it wanted. No consideration had been given to Ben's proposal that representatives from the colonies be allowed seats in Parliament.

A Red-Hot Poker

Some Parliament members, angry over the repeal of the Stamp Act, insisted that Americans pay for the government's costs in printing the millions of stamps, which were now worthless paper. Ben scoffed at this idea by publishing a zany, slightly naughty story in a London newspaper.

The idea of paying for the stamps, Ben said, put him in mind of the story of a Frenchman who brandished a red-hot poker at every Englishman he saw. Bowing politely, the Frenchman would say, "Pray do me the favor to let me have the honor of thrusting this hot iron into your backside."

"Zoons! What does this fellow mean?" the Englishman would cry. "Begone with your poker, or I shall break your head."

"Nay, sir," replied the Frenchman. "If you do not choose it, I do not insist upon it. But at least you will in justice have the goodness to pay me something for the heating of the iron."

A gruesome cartoon by Ben Franklin shows England separated from her colonies.

As tensions grew Ben tried to illustrate how vital the two countries were to each other by drawing, printing, and distributing this cartoon. It depicts Great Britain without four important limbs—New York, New England, Pennsylvania, and Virginia. In the background British ships have brooms tied to their masts, indicating they are for sale because of the loss of colonial trade. "England," fumed George III when he saw the cartoon, "may do as it wishes with its American colonies."

"WE HAVE AN OLD MOTHER"
A REVOLUTIONARY SONG

One day in 1773 Ben Franklin, colonial agent in London, wrote a song. Set to the tune of "Which Nobody Can Deny," a familiar British melody, he expressed the American colonies' feelings toward her "old mother country," England.

We have an old mother that
peevish is grown.
She snubs us like children that
scarce walk alone.
She forgets we're grown up and
have sense of our own.

Which nobody can deny, deny.
Which nobody can deny.

If we don't obey orders,
whatever the case;
She frowns and she chides,
and she loses all patience,
and sometimes she hits us
a slap in the face.

Which nobody can deny, deny.
Which nobody can deny.

Her orders so odd are,
we often suspect
That age has impaired
her sound intellect.
But still an old mother
should have some respect.

Which nobody can deny, deny.
Which nobody can deny.

We'll join her in lawsuits
to baffle all those
Who, to get what she has,
will be often her foes;
But we know it must all be
our own, when she goes.

Which nobody can deny, deny.
Which nobody can deny.

FROM BAD . . .

As colonial agent, Ben struggled to close the ever widening gap between England and the colonies. He hoped reason and common sense would return the two lands to a peaceful relationship. "As between friends, every affront is not worth a duel," he counseled, "between nations every injury is not worth a war." But Ben could not stop events from snowballing out of control.

1767

Parliament, believing the colonies exist solely for England's economic benefit, passes the Townshend Acts. One measure of the acts imposes heavy duties on glass, paper, tea, and other goods Americans buy from England.

Colonists, believing they should have the same rights as other Englishmen, call for a boycott of all English-made goods. They vow not to buy any of the newly taxed items until the Townshend Acts are repealed, while Bostonians riot in the streets.

Ben approves of the boycott, believing this economic pressure will force a change of attitude in London. At the present time, he says, "every man in this city seems to think himself a sovereign over America; seems to jostle himself into the throne with the king and talks of our subjects in the colonies."

This 1767 British cartoon satirizes America's resolve not to drink British tea or wear British-made clothes until the Townshend Acts are repealed by Parliament.

1768

Parliament sends troops to Boston to squash riots and the rising tide of revolutionary sentiment in that city.

Colonists heckle, tease, and insult the British soldiers.

Ben warns his British friends that having their troops on American soil could lead to violence. It "appears to me a dangerous step," he says. "It seems like setting up a [black]smith's forge in a magazine of gunpowder."

British troops land in Boston to squash American resistance.

. . . TO WORSE

This engraving of the Boston Massacre, created by Paul Revere and published in 1770, became a powerful piece of anti-British propaganda.

1770

Parliament, in hopes of appeasing angry colonists, repeals the Townshend Acts, except for the duty on tea. British soldiers—called redcoats by colonists because of the color of their uniforms—remain in Boston.

On March 5 a riot explodes in Boston. It begins with colonists pelting the redcoats with snowballs and ends with the soldiers opening fire on unarmed citizens. When the smoke clears, what will come to be known as the Boston Massacre is over, and five men lie dead in the snow.

The news, when it reaches London, deeply disturbs Ben. He is sad and angry—and growing pessimistic about the prospect of a peaceful settlement. "Those detestable cowards!" he says of the British soldiers. Then he adds, "Maintaining a standing army among us in time of peace, without our consent, is unconstitutional," referring to Britain's unwritten constitution, which curbs the power of the king and lays the foundation for representational government.

American colonists disguised as Native Americans smash open crates and dump tea into Boston Harbor.

1773

Parliament passes the Tea Act, making it illegal for Americans to buy their tea from any source but the British-owned East India Company. The act destroys America's tea trade. To add insult to injury, the government refuses to remove the duty from tea, claiming the money is needed to maintain troops in Boston.

Americans react by boycotting tea. But this action is not enough, and on December 16 a furious group of colonists disguised as Mohawk Indians board three English tea ships docked in Boston Harbor. With war whoops they toss 342 chests of tea overboard. The event is known as the Boston Tea Party.

Ben gives up nearly all hope of reconciliation. "I am at a loss to see how peace and union are to be restored," he says. Still, he denounces the tea party as an "act of violent injustice" and offers to pay for the ruined tea himself—*if* England will repeal the Tea Act and recognize American rights. England refuses.

1774

Parliament rams through a series of laws—called the Intolerable Acts by colonists and the Coercive Acts by the British—meant to punish Boston for the tea party. Boston Harbor is closed to all shipping until the ruined tea, plus the duty on it, is repaid. Town meetings are suspended. More soldiers are sent to Boston, and citizens are forced to house them in their own homes, at their own expense. To drive home the point, the commander in chief of the British army, Gen. Thomas Gage, is appointed by the king as Massachusetts's new governor. "We must control them, or submit to them!" declares England's prime minister.

Anger unites the colonists as never before. "An attack on one of our sister colonies is an attack made on all America!" they cry. Twelve of the thirteen colonies (Georgia went unrepresented) send delegates to a meeting in Philadelphia to decide what to do next. Known as the First Continental Congress, this gathering of delegates has a common goal—to agree on ways to defend America's rights.

What Ben sees and hears in London enrages him. "I have heard the government condemn Americans as the lowest of mankind, and almost of a different species from the British of England. They heap upon us both scorn, and contempt." He applauds the colonies' formation of a congress and changes his mind about paying for the ruined tea. "In my mind government should pay us for all the duties extorted by armed force!" Still, he makes a last-ditch effort to bring the two lands together by asking to speak before Parliament. His request is denied.

AMERICA in FLAMES.

This British cartoon, published in January 1775, pokes fun at the effects of the Coercive Acts on America.

In January 1774 Ben stands before the Privy Council, a group of nobles who advise the king.

The British ministry was furious over the Boston Tea Party. Calling Ben before them, they unleashed all their wrath on him. The lords and ladies were invited, "as to an entertainment," to watch with glee as the king's lawyer, Alexander Wedderburn, sneered, shouted, questioned Ben sarcastically, and called him names. For almost an hour Ben stood there enduring these abuses, while the room rocked with laughter and the lords of the Privy Council studied him with mocking, haughty eyes. "The whole time," said one eyewitness, "[Ben] remained like a rock, in the same posture, his chin resting on his left hand, and in that attitude abiding the pelting of the pitiless storm." But this silence did not mean Ben intended to forgive or forget such an outrage. As the meeting ended Ben found himself walking beside his tormenter. Taking him by the arm, Ben hissed in his ear, "I will make your master a little king for this." Ben had reached the point of despair and now believed war was inevitable. There was "nothing left for honest Americans in the [British] empire, but insult and condemnation," he wrote. He returned to Philadelphia fourteen months later.

A Game of Chess . . . and Politics

Ben would have returned to Philadelphia immediately after his insulting experience before the Privy Council if he had not been invited to play chess with Richard Howe, a prominent member of Parliament, and his sister, Lady Caroline Howe. He knew the meeting would be more than a table game. After several matches Lady Howe asked casually, "What is to be done with this dispute . . . ? How can America be satisfied?" Ben tried his best to interpret and make clear his country's position on the growing breach. Luckily his humor did not desert him. The answer, Ben replied, could be found in a few *res:*

RE {
-call your forces.
-store Castle William (in Boston Harbor).
-pair the damage done to Boston.
-peal your unconstitutional acts.
-nounce your pretentious taxes.
-fund the duties you have extorted; after this,
-quire payment for the destroyed tea,
AND THEN:
-joice in a happy
-conciliation.
}

THE COLONIAL AGENT'S LAST ACT

On March 21, 1775, before setting sail for Philadelphia, Ben spent several hours with his scientist friend Joseph Priestley going over newspapers recently arrived from America. From them Ben picked articles he hoped might win some sympathy for the colonies if they were republished in British newspapers. While doing so, his sense of failure overcame him.

"He was frequently not able to proceed," Mr. Priestley later wrote, "for the tears literally running down his cheeks."

AN EIGHTEENTH-CENTURY ENGRAVING SHOWS

THE BATTLE OF LEXINGTON—THE BEGINNING OF THE REVOLUTIONARY WAR.

Ben had barely set foot in Philadelphia when he heard the news—war had erupted! Just two weeks earlier, on April 19, 1775, British troops had headed toward Concord, Massachusetts, to take American supplies of gunpowder and weapons. But American patriot Paul Revere had warned colonists of the British on his now famous "midnight ride." Five miles from their destination, in the little town of Lexington, the Brits were met by an assemblage of sixty or seventy minutemen (a volunteer defense force that could be "ready in a minute"). "Lay down your arms and disperse!" ordered a British officer. The minutemen hesitated, then someone fired a musket. Each side would later claim that the other fired first. Although the fighting lasted only a few minutes, when the smoke cleared, eight Americans were dead and ten were wounded. While the stunned townspeople looked on, the British fired a victory shot, gave three cheers, and marched on toward Concord. American horsemen quickly carried the news of the bloodshed to nearby towns. When the British arrived in Concord, hundreds of minutemen were waiting for them. But they did not attack. Believing their munitions were safely hidden, and wanting to avoid bloodshed, they watched from a nearby hill as the redcoats began a house-to-house search. The British took the items they found, piled them in the street, and started a bonfire with them. Thinking they were burning the town, the minutemen charged down the hill and started to cross North Bridge into Concord. British soldiers tried to stop them, but the Americans kept coming. Muskets were fired and three British soldiers fell. The other redcoats panicked and ran. But as they retreated toward Boston, swarms of colonists appeared. They ambushed the British at every turn, firing from barns, from house windows, from behind stone walls. By the time the battered British army straggled into Boston, 272 of their men had been killed, wounded, or were missing, The Americans counted 94 casualties in all.

Ben, who had hoped to enjoy a well-deserved retirement, quickly changed his plans after hearing these details. "Nothing can save us from the most abject destruction," he wrote in a letter addressed to the public, "but a spirited opposition. It will be our salvation."

BEN'S CREDENTIALS
APPOINTING HIM TO THE
CONTINENTAL CONGRESS,
MAY 6, 1775

Less than twenty-four hours
after landing in Philadelphia,
Ben became a delegate to the
Second Continental
Congress—its oldest (he was
sixty-nine) and most
revolutionary delegate.
While most other members
of the congress refused to
discuss or even consider
independence from England,
Ben immediately declared
himself in favor of it. "Dr.
Franklin," John Adams
wrote, "is Britain's bitterest
foe. . . . He does not hesitate
at [Congress's] boldest
measures, but rather seems to
think us too irresolute and
backward." It would be
another whole year before
other congressional members
would agree with Ben that
America should be "free and
independent from England."

Ben Plunges into the Work of Revolution

Rising at five each morning, Ben attended as many as four meetings with various congressional committees before riding to the statehouse for eight hours of debate. During the next eighteen months he busied himself procuring arms and money for the army, drawing up plans for the naval defense of Philadelphia, reviewing troops, and organizing the Pennsylvania militia. Because the postal service was still run by the British government, letters from rebellious members of the Congress, or soldiers in the American army, were not delivered. Ben quickly organized a rival system. With Philadelphia as the central office, the postal route ran from Falmouth, New Hampshire, to Savannah, Georgia. Night riders delivered the mail within days, making the American postal service more efficient than the British one. The two post offices existed side by side for the next six months, until the British ended its service. For these postal efforts Congress unanimously elected Ben the postmaster general for the American colonies at a salary of a thousand dollars a year—a salary he gave away for the relief of wounded soldiers. "My time," Ben wrote, "has never been more fully occupied." No wonder John Adams noted that, during Congress, Ben was "a great deal of the time fast asleep in his chair."

Philadelphia's statehouse, circa 1930

THE VERY FIRST DECLARATION OF INDEPENDENCE

On June 17, 1775, a full-scale battle erupted north of Boston. The American army seized the high ground known as Breed's Hill and Bunker Hill, and redcoats attacked. More than four hundred Americans died, and some three hundred buildings were burned. This battle confirmed what Ben had believed—the need for American independence. So in July 1775, one whole year before Congress took that bold step, Ben wrote his own declaration of independence. Sadly, only one congressional delegate, Thomas Jefferson, responded enthusiastically. Others felt the proposal was too antagonistic toward the British. Did they really want to split from England, or should they retain their rights as Englishmen? That question would not be decided for another year.

> *Whereas the British nation, through great corruption of manners . . . have found all honest resources insufficient to supply their excessive luxury . . . and thereby have been driven to the practice of every injustice . . . and grudging us the fruits of our hard labour and virtuous industry, have for years been endeavoring to extort the same from us . . . And whereas they have proceeded to open robbery, declaring by a solemn act of Parliament that all our estates are theirs . . . And they have even dared to declare that all the spoiling, thefts, burnings of houses and towns and murders of innocent people, perpetrated by their wicked corsairs, previous to any war declared upon us, were just actions . . . thereby manifesting themselves to be enemies of mankind; And whereas it is not possible for the people of America to subsist under such continual ravages without making some reprisals: Therefore, Resolved &c.*

> *Benjamin Franklin*

GEN. GEORGE WASHINGTON, COMMANDER OF THE AMERICAN ARMY

ON JULY 2, 1775, the Second Continental Congress handed over command of the ragtag American army to George Washington, who quickly discovered he was heading up a poorly trained, underfed, ill-equipped collection of farmers and tradesmen. Washington appealed to the Congress for help; without it, he warned, the army would "disintegrate." They responded by appointing a committee, led by Ben, to investigate. In October 1775 Ben and two other delegates traveled to Washington's headquarters outside Boston. For seven days the men discussed rations: a pound of beef or salt fish, or three quarters of a pound of pork, per man per day; a pound of bread; a pint of milk or a quart of beer or cider. They determined army size: It should be increased from ten thousand to twenty thousand. They discussed weaponry: Gunsmiths should be set to work making firelocks with barrels three quarters of an inch in bore. "Details, details, details," Ben later wrote. While unimpressed by the state of the army, Ben was impressed by its leader. "I have no doubts of [Washington's] defending our people, their cities and country bravely," he said. The two men became lifelong friends.

Thomas Paine's radical pamphlet
Common Sense

In January 1776 many colonists still remained undecided about independence. While they opposed the war and Britain's harsh treatment of Americans, they still considered themselves subjects of the king. But Ben still firmly believed that independence was necessary and desperately wanted to sway people's opinion in favor of freedom. Then he read his friend Thomas Paine's bold essay in favor of independence. Never before had Ben heard such scorching sentiments so freely expressed. Paine called the king a "royal brute" and the monarchy "exceedingly ridiculous." The ties between England and America, he insisted, "sooner or later must end." Ben knew the essay had to be published. Having arranged for its printing, he watched as a stunning number of copies of *Common Sense* poured from the presses—an instant bestseller. Just as Ben had predicted, the "little pamphlet" formed opinion and changed minds. "I believe," Ben wrote the following spring, "that the country . . . is with us."

BEN IS APPOINTED TO THE COMMITTEE TO PREPARE A DECLARATION OF INDEPENDENCE

By June 1776 most members of the Second Continental Congress had agreed to consider the matter of independence. Thinking it might be a good idea to have a document ready, they chose five delegates to work on it—Thomas Jefferson, John Adams, Robert R. Livingston of New York, Roger Sherman of Connecticut, and Ben. Right away the newly formed committee wrangled over who should write the document. Adams refused, wisely recognizing that "people find me obnoxious, suspicious and unpopular." Sherman and Livingston were disqualified for more obvious reasons—Livingston was unsure about the idea of independence (he would later refuse to sign the finished document) and Sherman was no writer. Jefferson was finally picked because he had a "grave, and lofty style suitable to the occasion." One story says Ben wasn't chosen to write it because the Founding Fathers feared he'd slip in a joke or two. Actually, Ben probably would have written the declaration if the seventy-year-old had not been recovering from a case of the gout, accompanied by severe boils and a rash. Feeling as he did, Ben was happy to leave the task to the younger man.

JOHN ADAMS, NOT BEN'S BEST FRIEND

Although Ben and John Adams worked together, they did not like each other. Adams, worried about his own place in history, was jealous of Ben. "History will probably tell the story of the revolution," he snidely wrote in his diary, "by saying Franklin's electrical rod smote the earth and out sprang George Washington . . . Franklin electrified him with his rod, and hence forward those two conducted all the policy, negotiations, legislatures and wars!" As for Ben, he found Adams touchy and unreasonable. "[Adams] means well for his country, is always an honest man, often a wise one, but sometimes, and in some things, absolutely out of his senses."

THE ROUGH DRAFT OF THE DECLARATION OF INDEPENDENCE, EDITED BY BEN

When Thomas Jefferson finished writing, he sent the draft along to the Franklin house. "Will Dr. Franklin be so good as to peruse it and suggest . . . alterations?" Jefferson asked in an attached note. After years as a writer and printer Ben knew good prose when he read it. He treated Jefferson's writing gently, merely strengthening phrases and making minor word changes. The most memorable and enduring of these was to substitute the word "self-evident" for Jefferson's "sacred and undeniable" in that famous phrase—"We hold these truths to be self-evident; that all men are created equal."

Ben Tells Tom a Story

The Second Continental Congress did not treat Thomas Jefferson's Declaration of Independence as gently as Ben did. They debated and argued over words, sentences, and entire paragraphs. Jefferson sat through these debates, feeling angry, insulted, and a little embarrassed. Seeing his distress, Ben consoled him by telling this story.

When I was a journeyman printer one of my friends, an apprentice hatter . . . was about to open a shop for himself. His first concern was to have a handsome signboard with a proper inscription. He composed it in these words: "John Thompson, hatter, makes and sells hats for ready money"; with a figure of a hat subjoined. But he thought he would submit it to his friends for their amendments. The first he showed it to thought the word "Hatter," redundant. . . . It was struck out. The next observed that the word "makes" might well be omitted because his customers would not care who made the hats. . . . He struck it out. A third said he thought the words "for ready money" were useless as it was not the custom of the place to sell on credit. They were parted with, and the inscription now stood: "John Thompson, sells hats." "Sells hats!" says his next friend. "Why nobody would expect you to give them away. What then is the use of that word?" It was stricken out, and "hats" followed it . . . as there was one painted on the board. So the inscription was ultimately reduced to "John Thompson," with a figure of a hat subjoined.

BEN AND THE OTHER DELEGATES SIGN

AN ACT OF TREASON

On July 4, 1776, the Second Continental Congress voted on, and twelve colonies unanimously approved, Thomas Jefferson's Declaration of Independence. (New York abstained, its delegates claiming they had no directions from their constituents.) That afternoon the document was signed by John Hancock, president of the Congress. He wrote his name large enough, he said, for King George to read it without his glasses. Most historians believe no other delegates added their signatures until August 2, when the document had been copied onto a sheet of durable parchment. Then, one at a time, the delegates placed their signatures on the bottom. They knew they were risking everything—fortune, reputation, their very lives—for freedom. By putting their names on this revolutionary document, they were committing treason. And English law dealt harshly with traitors—they were hanged. At this sober moment Ben chose to make a joke. Said John Hancock, "We must be unanimous; there must be no pulling different ways; we must all hang together." "Yes," replied Ben. "We must all hang together, or most assuredly, we shall all hang separately." Altogether fifty-six men signed the Declaration of Independence.

THE DECLARATION OF INDEPENDENCE

THE FINAL VERSION OF THE DECLARATION OF INDEPENDENCE

What does this document say? It begins by explaining why the colonies decided to free themselves from British rule. "All men are created equal," Thomas Jefferson wrote. They have certain God-given freedoms, including the rights to "Life, Liberty, and the pursuit of Happiness." Governments are created to secure those rights for their citizens, the document states, but King George III violated these rights. The declaration then includes a long list of grievances against the king, including, "imposing taxes on us without our consent," "suspending our own legislatures," and "waging war against us." Governments must have the "consent of the governed," the document continues. If a government fails to protect its citizens' rights, its citizens have the right to change or abolish that government. Therefore, "the Representatives of the United States of America . . . do, in the Name, and by Authority of the good People of these Colonies, solemnly publish and declare That these United Colonies are, and of Right ought to be, Free and Independent States." For the first time, the name United States of America was used, the Continental Congress became known simply as the Congress, and a new nation was born. England, however, refused to recognize the newly independent nation. Declared King George III, "The die is now cast. The colonies must either submit or triumph." The king intended for them to submit.

BEN AND OTHER MEMBERS OF CONGRESS ANNOUNCE THE DECLARATION OF INDEPENDENCE.

On July 4, 1776, the Declaration of Independence was read to the public in Pennsylvania's statehouse yard. Wrote one eyewitness, "There were bonfires, ringing bells, and other great demonstrations of joy." Meanwhile, hastily printed copies of the document were carried by express riders and coastal schooners to towns and villages throughout what would now be called the thirteen states. In Boston crowds took to the street, singing and chanting. In New York City patriots pulled down the statue of King George III and dragged it away to be melted down for bullets. With independence declared, Ben felt there was "everything to be done, all at once, and much of it impossible." The war, which had been raging for more than a year, had to be won and a new, free nation created.

Ben's first-ever American political cartoon, reinterpreted for the times

Ben originally created this segmented snake in the 1750s to urge colonists to unite against the French and Native Americans. Americans, however, revived the cartoon when the war began. It was used as a warning of what could happen if the colonies did not work together to throw off English rule.

SOUVENIRS FROM FRANCE

> An old man of seventy, I undertook a winter sea voyage at the command of the Congress and for the public service with no other attendant to take care of me.

—Benjamin Franklin, letter to Richard Bache, 1781

BEN TAKES THE WAR TO FRANCE

Just weeks after the Declaration of Independence was signed, Gen. George Washington and the American army were forced by British redcoats to abandon their position on Long Island, leaving New York City to the British. A devastating defeat, it convinced Congress of the desperate need for help. Members voted to send Ben to France. Together with two other Americans awaiting him in Paris (Silas Deane and Arthur Lee), Ben's mission was to get whatever he could: gifts and loans of money, supplies, ships, ammunition, trained army officers, and if possible, an alliance at war.

For a man of seventy-one suffering from gout and other afflictions, leaving his home to cross a wintry sea patrolled by enemy ships was no small undertaking. Still, Ben had made the decision that America must be free, and he was determined to give his all. "I am resolved to devote myself to the work that my fellow citizens deem necessary; or speaking as old-clothes dealers do of a remnant of goods, 'You shall have me for what you please.'" With much sadness, believing his old age would keep him from ever returning home, Ben bid farewell to Philadelphia.

"Figure to yourself an old man with gray hair appearing under a marten fur cap, among the powdered heads of Paris." This was how Ben described himself soon after arriving in France in December 1776. He hoped to win aid for the faltering American Revolution and knew that much of his support would have to come from the people. Understanding the value of image, Ben made a point of wearing the fur hat, along with a plain brown suit. Declared one excited

BEN WEARING HIS SOON-TO-BE-FAMOUS FUR HAT

Frenchman, "Everything about him announces the simplicity and innocence of primitive morals. . . . The people clustered around him and asked: 'Who is this old peasant who has such a noble air?'" The frill-and-lace-loving French saw his wardrobe as proof that Americans were simple and honest—so unlike the shrewd and sophisticated British. Ben and his hat became a public relations coup, a first big step in winning French support for independence.

ANOTHER COUNTRY, ANOTHER KING

Portrait of King Louis XVI

When he arrived in Paris, Ben found a country of sharp contrasts. "There is . . . in [France] a prodigious mixture of magnificence and neglect," he observed, "with every kind of elegance except that of cleanliness and what we would call charitable kindness."

Indeed, the streets of Paris were loud, dirty, and often unsafe. Peddlers crowded the narrow, trash-strewn boulevards, hawking their wares, while pickpockets preyed on unsuspecting passersby, and prostitutes hung about in doorways. Most disturbing was evidence of Paris's poverty. Wrote one visitor, "Everywhere one looks the blind, the lame, the poor (for there are many!) hold out battered, copper bowls, begging."

Unlike the "hard and miserable life" of the common man was the lifestyle of the aristocracy. The aristocracy loved leisure. They emphasized style over substance. They were lavish, sophisticated, and frivolous.

These qualities were typified by their twenty-three-year-old ruler, King Louis XVI. Fat and sluggish, Louis had little interest in running his country. Instead he turned his attention to more pleasurable pursuits—napping, hunting, and entertaining. In his vast palace at Versailles he and his wife, Marie Antoinette, lived in splendor. Waited on by hundreds of servants, they ate off gold plates, wore jewel-encrusted clothing, and often threw lavish public dinners for as many as ten thousand guests. Observed one visitor, "Both the king, and his subjects are most sinfully extravagant."

Members of the aristocracy often stayed out until dawn,

One powdered head of Paris with an added special touch

attending the opera or theater, or gathering at a friend's home to sing, dance, or gamble. Witty, intelligent conversation was a must at these events, and men and women "flirted shame-lessly." After attending one such gathering, Ben wrote, "Somebody gave it out that I loved the ladies, and then everybody presented me with their ladies to be embraced."

Some Americans saw this behavior as proof of France's loose morals. The French, declared John Adams, "have a

Ben surrounded by the fashionable and flirtatious French ladies

tendency toward idleness . . . they seldom rise from their beds before noon, and when they do . . . they merely begin anew the ritual of powdering, primping and attending parties. . . . It is a wonder anything is done at all!"

But Ben felt differently. "The French . . . are harmless," he wrote. "To dress their heads so that a hat cannot be put on them, and then wear their hats under their arms may be called follies, perhaps, but they are not vices. . . . In short, there is nothing wanting in the character of a Frenchman, that belongs to that of an agreeable and worthy man."

The palace at Versailles, the most opulent in all of Europe

B E N ' S   H O M E   I N   F R A N C E

Ben lived in hotels for a brief time when he first arrived in Paris in December 1776. By spring, however, he had moved to a little village just outside the city, called Passy. His landlord, a rich shipping merchant named Monsieur Brillon, rented Ben a wing of his luxurious manor. There Ben lived like an aristocrat. He kept nine servants, a coachman with horse and carriage, and a cellar filled with expensive wines. He ate well too, as his "accounts and waistline prove[d]," he wrote. When John Adams witnessed this lavish lifestyle, he was shocked. But Ben simply replied that frugality was "a virtue [he] never could acquire in [him]self." Besides, didn't he "save quite a bit by dining out as a guest six days out of seven?"

A British newspaper published this cartoon about Ben.

Ben's arrival in France caused London to buzz with rumor, speculation, and worry. Londoners knew Ben Franklin. They respected his abilities. But could he really sway France to the American cause? The British newspapers thought so, and they published this cartoon, called "The Plan." It shows Ben (center) holding a copy of the plan for the French invasion of England in one hand, and strings that are connected to the noses of the king of France and his cabinet in the other. Yes, the newspapers seemed to say, Ben Franklin could achieve just about anything.

Only a Stormont

Lord Stormont, the British ambassador in France, desperately wanted the French to mistrust Ben. So he went about Paris telling all sorts of wild stories about the American. Stormont claimed Ben was a magician who had hypnotized the king's advisers. He claimed Ben was working with other world scientists to create weapons of mass destruction. He even suggested Ben was trying to weave all of Europe into one nation with himself as king. These fibs inspired Ben to one of his best witticisms.

One day a French friend rushed to Ben. He had heard Lord Stormont's latest fib. "Six battalions of American armies have surrendered!" the Frenchman reported. "Is it true?"

"Oh, no," replied Ben. "It is only a Stormont."

Within a day Ben's comment had swept Paris, and *Stormonter* became a new French slang word meaning "to lie." Stormont himself grew so agitated over this that one day he wrote no less than nine letters to London about Ben's "nefarious activities."

BEN'S IMAGE, AS ENGRAVED ON THIS MEDAL, APPEARED ALL OVER FRANCE.

Ben's popularity in Paris soared, and his face became the symbol of the revolutionary era. "My face is as well known as the moon," he wrote to his daughter, Sally. "Incredible numbers of my pictures are sold." He was not exaggerating. His likeness soon decorated everything imaginable—rings, mirrors, medals, handkerchiefs, pocketknives—even chamber pots! When John Adams arrived in Paris, he grudgingly admitted the tremendous impact Ben had had on the French people. "His name is familiar . . . to such a degree that there is scarcely a peasant or a citizen . . . a coachman, or footman, a lady's chambermaid, or a scullion in the kitchen who is not familiar with it, and who does not consider [Dr. Franklin] a friend to humankind."

ARTHUR LEE, THE MAN BEN CALLED HIS "MOST MALICIOUS ENEMY"

One of the three men appointed by Congress to enlist help from France—the other two were Ben and Silas Deane, a Connecticut politician who was already in Paris trying to buy wartime supplies—Lee was bitter and bad tempered. He falsely accused Ben of stealing money and withholding important information, and claimed Ben's grandson Temple was a British spy—allegations he passed on to Congress. For the sake of the mission Ben tried to ignore Lee's insults and lies. But eventually he exploded in anger. "If I have borne your snubbings and rebukes," he steamed, "it is only out of pity for your sick mind which is forever tormenting itself with its jealousies, suspicions, and fancies that others mean you ill will. . . . If you do not cure yourself of this temper it will end in insanity. . . . God preserve you from so terrible an evil; and for His sake, pray suffer me to live in quiet!" Ben's prayers were answered in 1778 when Congress appointed him the sole minister plenipotentiary (a position similar to our modern-day ambassador), and requested that Lee return to America. Even then Lee's tongue did not stop wagging. In Congress he railed about the "evil Dr. Franklin." But his ranting went ignored.

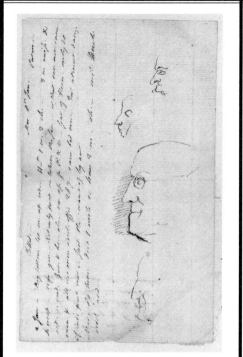

Ben's grandson sketched him in his notebook.

Ben did not arrive in France alone. Accompanying him were two grandsons, seventeen-year-old Temple Franklin (William's son), and seven-year-old Benny Bache (Sally's son). While Temple stayed in Paris working as his grandfather's secretary, Benny went to school in Switzerland, returning only on holidays and special occasions. On one such occasion, a dinner party, he drew a profile sketch of Ben. Later he told this story: His grandfather, Benny said, had trouble with the French language, especially when it was spoken. At this particular party there were many rapidly spoken speeches. Unable to understand them, Ben watched the woman beside him. When she clapped, he clapped. When she whooped, he whooped. Hoping to appear friendly, he made sure he clapped, and whooped more loudly than anyone else. Benny, who understood French much better than his grandfather, finally leaned over and whispered in the old man's ear. "Imagine grandpapa's embarrassment," Benny later wrote, "when he learned he had been applauding praises of himself all night!"

Mission Impossible

The French people sympathized with Americans, but their minister of foreign affairs, the comte de Vergennes, worried that France lacked the financial resources to fight a war with England. He decided to wait and see. If the Americans successfully resisted the English and made clear they were an ally worth having in a war, France would join them. If, on the other hand, America appeared weak, France would stay out of the fray. Ben understood this policy and privately felt his mission to France was "impossible and doomed" because of America's many losses in battle. Still, he was publicly optimistic, and he blithely assured French officials that all talk of British victories was nonsense by telling less-than-accurate stories like this one:

> I see you [French officials] have had bad news of our affairs in America, but they are not true. . . . The British have . . . gained a footing on two islands [Manhattan and Long Island!] but that is all. They have not extended their foothold on the continent.

A SKETCH OF BEN KISSING A YOUNG LADY WHO SITS ON HIS KNEE

Through the years Ben kissed many women. As one of his friends claimed, Ben could "with equal ease charm the lightning and the ladies." In France one of Ben's favorites was Madame Brillon, the wife of his landlord. Twice a week Ben visited that family to play chess, drink tea, and flirt with Madame. She called him *"mon cher papa"* and formed "the sweet habit" of sitting on Ben's lap. She also wrote him poetry and affectionate letters. Her husband approved of this behavior—flirting was, after all, a common and acceptable behavior among members of the French aristocracy. Monsieur Brillon knew that the relationship between his wife and the esteemed, elderly American was simply harmless fun. Sometimes he even joined in. Once after finding Ben and Madame alone in the sitting room, he declared, "I am certain you have just been kissing my wife, my dear doctor. Allow me to kiss you back!"

BEN AND ANNE-CATHERINE: A LOVE STORY

On a summer day in 1777 a friend invited Ben to join him at another friend's estate. Ben agreed. And what he saw there astonished him. The grounds blazed with bright-colored rhododendrons, roses, and poppies. Deer, ducks, dogs, and cats roamed free and were obviously well loved. Inside the house chaos and disorganization ruled. Papers lined the sofas. Dirty stockings lay on the carpet. Into this scene burst the owner of the estate, the widow Madame Anne-Catherine Helvétius.

Observed one guest, "She was jaunty, careless. Her hair was frizzled; over it she had a small, straw hat with a dirty handkerchief behind. . . . She ran forward [and] caught [Ben] by the hand. '*Helas*, Franklin!' she cried, then gave him a double kiss, one upon each cheek, and another upon the forehead."

Ben, who had been a widower for almost three years, was instantly dazzled by this over-fifty woman with her rollicking abandon of manners and dress. From then on he visited her every chance he got. Using a combination of French and English, the two discussed books, music, philosophy. She playfully called him "Franklin" and sent him notes like this one: "Do you want, my dear, to have dinner with me . . . ? I have the greatest desire to see you and embrace you."

He lovingly called her "Helvétia" and replied: "Of course I shall come. I get too much pleasure from holding you in my arms."

Eventually Ben proposed to her. But Madame Helvétius wanted to remain faithful to the memory of her husband and refused. Ben then wrote her a story in hopes of changing her mind. He told her he had dreamed of dying and going to heaven. There he met Monsieur Helvétius who gravely told Ben he had found a new wife in paradise. At that moment the wife appeared. Ben was amazed to learn it was Deborah, his wife on Earth. "Come," he suggested to Madame Helvétius after telling her the dream's details. "Let us revenge ourselves." Madame still said no.

Ben's feelings were hurt by her refusal. Still, the two remained close. When the day finally came for him to return to America, Madame begged him to stay. "Come back, *mon cher ami*," she cried. "Come back!"

But though Ben returned to Philadelphia, his heart was always with her. "I miss my share of your lovely, sensible talk," he wrote her, "and the wit and the love with which your meals were always seasoned."

"I will always love you," she wrote back. "We are not fated to meet again in this world. Well, my dear friend, let it be in the next."

The final words were his—written in a rusty French that conveyed a last message of longing. "Often in my dreams," he wrote, " I have breakfast with you. I sit beside you on one of your thousand sofas. I walk with you in your beautiful garden."

Philadelphia Occupied

In November 1777 grim news arrived in Paris: The British had captured Philadelphia. Ben's family, friends, and home now rested in enemy hands. Sick over the fate of his family, anxious over the future of the country, Ben felt every one of his seventy-one years. Still, he refused to show his anguish, displaying instead his wit.

"Well, Doctor Franklin," said one dinner guest mockingly. "I hear [British] General Howe has taken Philadelphia."

"I beg your pardon," replied Ben with an arch smile. "But Philadelphia has taken General Howe."

THE PLIGHT OF AMERICAN PRISONERS OF WAR, LIKE THE ONES SHOWN IN THIS ENGRAVING, RALLIED BEN TO ACTION.

American sailors captured off the British coast were routinely tossed into cold, cramped, rat-infested prisons where they were given little clothing and even less food. This appalling treatment of American citizens distressed Ben. Even though Congress had not authorized him to do so, he pressed for their release. But the British government refused. So Ben turned to other, less legal methods. Using his own money, he bribed guards and paid sympathizers to help the men escape to France. He set up a fund to feed and clothe them once they arrived. And he lobbied American officials to pay for their passage back to America. "It is not trifles that will do for men who come naked by the dozen," he wrote. "It is harder still to turn one's back on them."

SPIES, SPIES, AND MORE SPIES

Just three weeks after Ben arrived in France, an American widow living in Paris sent him a warning: "You are surrounded with spies!"

Ben shrugged. "It is impossible to prevent being watched by spies when interested people place them for that purpose," he said. So he created a rule for himself, "to do nothing that I should blush to have made public."

Ben followed his rule. And British spies followed him. Anxious to learn about his negotiations with France, they searched Ben's rooms, read his mail, and kept track of all his movements. They even planted one of their secret agents in Ben's home. But Ben knew his butler was really a spy, and so this spy-turned-servant uncovered little information. In one instance, however, he did report the state of Ben's underwear as being incredibly clean and "very white."

Underwear, however, did not interest the British. So they sent in their master spy— Edward Bancroft. Bancroft had known Ben in London. When the war began, Ben had asked him to send the Americans "information of what is going on in England." In other words, Ben asked Bancroft to spy for the Americans. Bancroft agreed, and Congress voted him a salary for his services. When Ben arrived in France, Bancroft came to stay with him in his home. He helped Ben write letters, kept track of accounts, and provided tidbits of information on British activities. And all the while he spied on Ben. "The role of double agent," Bancroft later said, "was repugnant to me." But the money he received from the British "assuaged [his] distaste."

For the next year Bancroft lived with Ben and relayed many of the Americans' secrets. "I regularly reported on every transaction; of every step and vessel taken to supply the revolted colonies; of every part of his intercourse with the French; of all the powers and instructions given by Congress; and all their secret correspondence," the spy later admitted. Writing his reports in invisible ink, he placed them in a sealed bottle, which he then left in the knothole of a tree. At exactly half past nine every Tuesday evening a messenger picked up Bancroft's report and left an empty bottle for future communications.

But little did Bancroft know that he, too, was being watched. The French had spies as well, and they were keeping an eye on British spies. Of course, American spies were keeping an eye on French and British spies. And British spies were on the lookout for American and French spies.

It was a tangled web of espionage, one which Ben refused to get trapped in—that is, until news of Gen. Horatio Gates's victory at Saratoga. The French had long promised to join in the fight for freedom if the American army could prove its ability to defeat the British. But despite this victory at Saratoga, the French balked.

Knowing how badly Americans needed French aid, Ben decided to use a bit of espionage himself and invited the head of the British Secret Service, Paul Wentworth, to his home for dinner. Wentworth eagerly accepted. That evening Ben talked and talked and talked but said nothing of importance. Said Wentworth, "I never knew him to be so eccentric."

But Ben was simply putting on a show for the French spies who he knew were watching. They reported the dinner between the American and the British official, and the French began to fret. Were the two sides trying to reach a compromise? Had France played the "wait and see" game too long? French officials saw their chance of humbling Britain fading away. They saw their dreams of a profitable trade policy with America evaporating. They had to do something— quick! The very next morning King Louis's council voted in favor of an alliance. At last France would join America in the fight for freedom. And Ben grinned. "Spies," he later wrote, "can be very useful."

The war seen from France

Although Ben no longer had firsthand knowledge of the war raging in America, he did receive reports from home. News was dismal. "Surely," he said privately to one French friend, "America's virtue and bravery can produce one victory."

It finally did. On the morning of December 4, 1777, a messenger arrived with news from America. "Sir!" cried the messenger, "General Burgoyne and his whole [British] army are prisoners of war!" The messenger then told Ben how the American general Horatio Gates defeated the British army in October at Saratoga, forcing them to lay down their weapons and surrender. Ben was overjoyed and spread word of the victory all across Europe. France was now convinced America was a worthy ally.

General Washington and his troops abandon Long Island to the British.

On February 6, 1778, the Treaty of Alliance Is Signed

Ben (center), along with (from left) Americans Silas Deane and Arthur Lee, and the French minister for foreign affairs, the comte de Vergennes (seated)

At last France was joining America's fight for independence. With a few strokes of a pen, the alliance became official. When Lord Stormont, the British ambassador, heard the news, he slunk out of Paris without paying his respects to the king, a breach of etiquette that practically declared war. Back in England, Parliament desperately offered the American Congress a deal. It would remove British troops and abolish oppressive taxes if America promised to remain part of the British Empire. But it was too little too late. A few months later French and British fleets clashed in the English Channel. By June 1779, Spain had joined the fighting, and a year later Holland declared war on England. The struggle for America's liberty had spread across Europe.

A Literary Snub

One day Ben happened to find himself eating lunch at the same French inn as Edward Gibbon, the well-known historian and author of *The History of the Decline and Fall of the Roman Empire* . . . and a Brit. Thrilled, Ben invited the historian to join him. This is what happened.

"A servant of the king," replied Gibbon, "cannot have a conversation with a rebel." Too bad, replied Ben, because if Gibbon ever decided to write a book on the decline and fall of the British Empire, Ben would be happy to supply the historian with "ample materials."

A Bareheaded Ben Meets King Louis XVI of France

With the Treaty of Alliance signed, the king of France finally recognized America as an independent nation and Ben as its official ambassador. Still portraying the simple American, Ben arrived at the king's court wearing a dark suit, white stockings, and plain shoes. Most stunning of all, he chose not to wear a wig. The sight of this wigless American sent the royal chamberlain, the man in charge of approved court dress, into shock. But when he protested, Ben laughed. "Dear boy, what matters is what you have inside your head, not on it!" he said. Then he strode into the king's room, where he assured the ruler of America's loyalty, friendship, and gratitude.

RECOMMENDING A PERSON YOU DO NOT KNOW

Day after day European men thronged Ben's office, begging to be made officers in the American army. Few of them had military experience. Most were simply bored young men in search of adventure. The never-ending crush of these requests, however, exasperated Ben. One day, after responding to his twenty-third application, he wrote this all-occasion letter, which he used to shame people who were making "especially ridiculous requests."

Sir:
The bearer of this letter who is going to America presses me to give him a letter of recommendation, though I know nothing of him, not even his name. This may seem extraordinary, but I assure you it is not uncommon here. Sometimes indeed one unknown person brings me another equally unknown person, to recommend him; and sometimes they recommend one another! As to this gentleman, I must refer you to himself for his character and merits, with which he is certainly better acquainted than I can possibly be.

*The **Bonhomme Richard** battles the **Serapis**—the result of a naval scheme hatched by Ben.*

In 1779 Ben became involved in a military plan to raid the English coastline. He was acquainted with John Paul Jones, a captain in the American navy who had already earned the designation "scourge of British shipping" because of his bold attacks on English vessels. Now Ben arranged for Jones to get a bigger ship, which the sailor named *Bonhomme Richard* in Ben's honor (*bonhomme* meaning "good man," and *Richard* from *Poor Richard's Almanack*; it became Ben's Paris nickname). Ben instructed Jones to keep a close eye on the British prisoners he held and not allow his crew (many of whom were recently escaped American prisoners of war) to hurt them. "And remember," added Ben, "though the English have wantonly burned many defenseless towns in America, you are not to follow their example." With this sound advice Jones sailed across the channel to England. On September 23 he encountered the British frigate *Serapis*. After a long and bloody battle Jones captured it, sending a stunning news flash across Europe: The Americans had beaten a British frigate in its home waters! Commented Ben, "Few actions at sea have demonstrated such steady, cool, determined bravery."

FRANCE TO THE RESCUE

After France joined the war, their officials were shocked to discover the true state of the Revolution. Washington's army consisted of only 3,000 hungry men, many without shoes, most without weapons. Wrote one soldier, "Instead of having wagons filled with provisions, we have a scant pittance. . . . Instead of full regiments we scarcely fill a field. . . . And instead of the prospect of glorious victory, we have gloom and bewilderment. Our dream of independence is dying."

France worked quickly to save that dream. Even before signing the Treaty of Alliance, the French had loaned America millions of dollars. Now the door to the French treasury was flung wide open. Ships. Ammunition. Uniforms. All were purchased with French money. By war's end in 1783 France found itself bankrupt—"Bankrupt," wrote one Frenchman, "for the sake of American freedom." Ironically, this bankruptcy would, within a few short years, trigger the bloody and historic French Revolution.

But France provided more than money. It immediately sent a fleet of warships and an army of 10,000 trained soldiers to America. Toward the end of the war France's fighting forces outnumbered America's two to one, and close to 1,500 were killed in action. Said Ben with heartfelt appreciation for France's contribution, "It's not possible to repay what I, and every other American, owe the glorious nation of France."

THE WAR ENDS WITH THE BATTLE OF YORKTOWN, OCTOBER 9-19, 1781

British general Charles Cornwallis surrenders the British army to Gen. George Washington at Yorktown, Virginia. It is the final battle of the Revolutionary War.

In America, Gen. George Washington and the French commander Comte de Rochambeau marched south and surrounded the British army at Yorktown, Virginia. The British, commanded by Gen. Charles Cornwallis, thought to escape by water, but the French fleet foiled their plan by sailing down the coast. Pounded relentlessly for ten days by allied guns, Cornwallis finally surrendered the British army. It was the last battle of the Revolution. Americans rejoiced.

In the eight years of the American Revolution, approximately 7,000 Americans were killed in action, 10,000 died in army camps of diseases like smallpox and dysentery, and about 8,500 died as prisoners. Battles (there were a total of 1,331 engagements on land and sea) were fought as far north as Canada and as far south as Georgia.

In England there was disbelief. "Oh God," said the British prime minister when he heard the news. "Oh God. It is all over. It is all over."

In France the news took Ben by surprise. Even more surprising, he learned he would be responsible for bringing the war to an end. When he wrote to Congress begging to retire, he was instead placed on the committee to negotiate a peace treaty with England. Said Ben simply, "I will endeavor to do my best."

An unfinished portrait of the American peace commission: (from left) John Jay, John Adams, Ben Franklin, Henry Laurens, and Ben's grandson and sometime secretary, Temple Franklin

The Peacemakers

In 1781 Congress chose these men to negotiate peace with England. It would be a difficult task. For two whole years the Americans and the British met in Paris to wrangle over issues. The British offered "limited independence." Americans refused. Americans demanded compensation for destroyed property, special fishing and trading rights, and an apology from Parliament. British commissioners fumed. More than once negotiations came close to breaking off. After one particularly heated meeting with the British commissioners, Ben turned to John Adams and, quoting from the New Testament of the Bible, said, "'Blessed are the peacemakers' is, I suppose, to be understood in the other world, for in this one they are frequently cursed."

Capturing a King

Ben loved the game of chess and spent many a French evening in play. It was during one of these matches that he made one of his best-known quips.

One night Ben played chess with the king's sister the Duchess of Bourbon. When the duchess, an inexpert player, illegally placed her own king in check, Ben illegally captured it. "Sir," declared the duchess, "in France we do not take kings so." Ben grinned.

"We do in America," he said.

ABIGAIL ADAMS, WHO CHANGED HER OPINION OF BEN

Abigail, wife of John Adams, first met Ben just before independence was declared. Charmed by him, she wrote, "I could . . . read in his countenance the virtues of his heart, among which patriotism shone in its full luster, and with that is blended every virtue of a Christian." But how quickly minds are changed. Just a few years later John was appointed by Congress to the American peace commission in Paris. Straitlaced Abigail joined him and was shocked by everything French—food, fashions, forms of entertainment. But most appalling was the way the French women had taken to "old doctor Franklin." She could not believe her eyes when they flung their arms around his neck, kissed him, and patted him! And what did Dr. Franklin do? He returned their petting, praising them as the best women in the world! "I own I was highly disgusted," declared Abigail. Dr. Franklin, she decided, was a "wicked, unprincipled, debauched wretch . . . an old deceiver!" Abigail maintained this new opinion to the end of her days.

The bald eagle, which became an American symbol against Ben's advice

"I wish the bald eagle had not been chosen as the representative of our country," he said when he heard of Congress's 1782 decision. "He is a bird of bad moral character; he does not get his living honestly. You may have seen him, perched on some dead tree, where, too lazy to fish for himself, he watches the labor of the fishing hawk; and when that diligent bird has at length taken a fish and is bearing it to his nest in support of his mate and young ones, the bald eagle pursues him, and takes it from him." What bird did Ben prefer? "The turkey," he declared, "is a respectable bird, and a true, original native of America."

THE TREATY OF PARIS

Finally, in September 1783, the English swallowed hard and agreed to a compromise. They would pay for all the seaports and homes they had destroyed in the United States if America promised to pay for any homes and businesses they had seized from loyalists. Under the terms of the treaty England recognized the independence of the United States and promised to maintain a "firm and perpetual peace" with the new nation. England also agreed to withdraw all troops from the United States without taking or destroying anything and provide Americans with fishing rights off the coast of Canada (a territory still controlled by Britain). Ben, along with John Adams and John Jay, signed the treaty on behalf of the United States; David Hartly, a member of Parliament, signed for England. (France would sign a separate peace treaty with England later that same day.) When it was done, Ben felt overwhelmed with joy. The war was officially over! Independence was officially won! Later that day seventy-seven-year-old Ben flung his arms around a French friend and whooped, "My friend! Could I have hoped at my age to enjoy such happiness?"

A FEW WORDS ABOUT PEACE

Shortly after the signing of the peace treaty Ben wrote these words to an old friend.

We are now friends with England and with all mankind. May we never see another war! For in my opinion there never was a good war or a bad peace.

A 1783 ENGRAVING OF THE BALLOON DEMONSTRATION THAT DELIGHTED BEN.

Ben's days in France were not all diplomacy and dinner parties. On September 19, 1783, he attended the first-ever launching of a hot-air balloon. Too ill to walk to the balloon site, he got as close as he could by carriage. With a small telescope he watched, enthralled, as the balloon sailed over the city. Later he sent a detailed report of this flight to his fellow scientists in England and America. Many of them bemoaned the expense and time—it took two days and nights to fill a balloon with heated air and hydrogen—and demanded to know what was the point of ballooning, what good did it do the average man? Ben, fore-seeing the day when people would be able to fly everywhere, replied, "What good is a newborn baby?"

In 1784 a physician named Friedrich Anton Mesmer claimed he could—through the use of séances, hypnosis, and electrically charged magnets—channel an invisible fluid from the "celestial heavens" to humans. Calling this fluid "animal magnetism" because of its "attraction to warm-blooded creatures," Mesmer promised to cure any illness, as well as speak to the dead. His practices quickly gained a large following, especially among wealthy Parisian wid-ows. When French officials learned Mesmer had earned hundreds of thousands of dollars, they grew suspicious and asked Ben to investigate. Under Ben's keen, scientific eye people with ailments ranging from asthma to tumors received the

A French cartoon shows Ben vanquishing the theory of animal magnetism.

"Mesmeric technique"—that is, Dr. Mesmer placed mag-nets on their bodies and spoke in hypnotic tones. But none were cured. Ben pub-lished his report. The theory of animal magnetism, he claimed, was not proved, and its practice should be discour-aged. Newspapers of the time printed Ben's report, and one even included this cartoon showing Ben and others delivering a copy to Mesmer. The document is shown radiating a magnetic force all its own that overturns Mesmer's equip-ment, scares his patients, and sends Mesmer (on the broomstick) and his associates fleeing from the scene. Dr. Mesmer and his techniques soon disap-peared from Paris.

A FRENCH FAREWELL

Ben had considered remaining in France after retiring from his position as ambassador. His friends, he wrote to Sally, "press me to stay . . . they . . . universally esteem and love me." Still, Ben chose to spend the "little remainder of [his] life with [his] family," and in July of 1785 he set out for the harbor and his waiting ship. Queen Marie Antoinette loaned him her royal litter (a sort of curtained couch) pulled by two large mules. Several of his friends, most notably a count, a cardinal, and a colonel, accompanied him to the sea. At every town and village along the route he was greeted with cheers and flowers. And at the Academy of Rouen he was presented with a magic square said to represent his name in numbers. ("I have perused it since," he wrote, "but do not comprehend it.") Finally the procession reached the harbor. Wrote Ben sorrowfully, "We shall stay here a few days . . . and then we shall leave France, the country I love most in the world. . . . I am not sure I will be happy in America, but I must go back." Days later he boarded a ship bound for England and then America, leaving behind a country full of heavy hearts.

FINAL REMEMBRANCES

Life, like a dramatic piece, should not only be conducted with regularity, but should finish handsomely. Being now in the last act, I begin to cast about for something fit to end with . . . I am very desirous of concluding on a bright point.

—BENJAMIN FRANKLIN, LETTER TO GEORGE WHITEFIELD, 1756

BEN'S PHILADELPHIA HOMECOMING

On September 14, 1785, after nine long years abroad, a light breeze carried Ben's ship into full view of what he called in his diary "dear Philadelphia!" News of his arrival had reached the city before Ben did, and as he landed at Market Street an enormous crowd lined the road, roaring a joyous welcome. Cannons boomed. Tears flowed. The huge crowd watched with delight as Sally hugged her father at the front door of his house. It was a triumphant homecoming. That night Ben closed his travel diary by writing, "God be praised and thanked for all his mercies."

PORTRAIT OF THE PRESIDENT OF PENNSYLVANIA, BEN FRANKLIN

Ben had barely settled back into American life when Pennsylvania's leaders came calling. They begged him to accept the position of president of Pennsylvania (a position much like our modern-day governor). Ben agreed. Less than a week later he found himself the leader of his state once again. When a friend asked him why he had accepted such a job at the age of seventy-nine, Ben replied, "I had not sufficient firmness to refuse their request." Although ill, and often bedridden, Ben served as his state's president for three years.

THE FIRST GOVERNMENT

After the Declaration of Independence was written and signed in 1776, the newly named United States of America needed a plan of government. It settled on the Articles of Confederation, a "league of friendship" between the thirteen states that provided for "their common defense, the securities of their liberties, and their mutual and general welfare." The articles created a national congress with the authority over military and foreign affairs. But this newly created Congress had no power over individual states. Under the articles each state kept its own freedoms and independence—in effect, each state was like its own country. Congress could not levy taxes or regulate trade. Its money came solely from how much each state decided to give. Often states chose to give nothing at all. Still, Congress played an important role during the Revolutionary War. It built and maintained an army, it established a wartime postal system, and it approved treaties and alliances.

But after winning independence, Congress's importance dwindled. Without the threat of the British, unity between the states no longer seemed necessary. Each went about its own business, printing its own money and making its own laws. Forgotten, the national Congress wandered from Princeton to Trenton to New York City in search of a permanent home. More often than not, members sat around for weeks waiting for missing delegates to appear. Without a source of revenue the penniless Congress could only watch the bills pile up. It could not afford a real army to stop invasions. And it certainly could not afford to pay the millions of dollars America owed in war debts.

England showed its contempt for this weak government by refusing to withdraw its troops from six forts on American soil. And pirates, knowing of the United States' lack of an effective navy, made it their policy to capture all American ships in the Mediterranean.

"I am mortified," said George Washington. "To be more exposed in the eyes of the world, and more contemptible than we already are, is hardly possible." He sent a letter to the governors of the thirteen states calling for a constitutional convention to meet in Philadelphia. Its purpose would be to reform the federal government.

In Philadelphia, Ben strongly backed the convention and worried about its outcome. "If it does not do good, it must do harm," he wrote, "for it will show we have not the wisdom enough among us to govern ourselves." With the eyes of the world watching, America set out to form a new government.

Ben, the oldest delegate to the Constitutional Convention

From May until September 1787 fifty-five delegates from every state except Rhode Island (which simply chose not to send delegates) worked to forge our Constitution—a document that would create a new government

for America. Among these delegates were Alexander Hamilton of New York, who passionately wanted the convention to succeed; James Madison of Virginia, whose contributions to the convention would earn him the nickname "Father of the Constitution"; and Elbridge Gerry of Massachusetts, dubbed the "Grumbletonian" because he found so much fault with the convention. Eighty-one-year-old Ben was not only the oldest delegate, but its most famous one as well. Because of this many people thought he should be president of the convention. But Ben had other ideas. Concerned his health would not stand the wear and tear of the daily sessions, and convinced that the project would have better success under the

leadership of his old friend George Washington, Ben bowed out of the running. "It was a graceful gesture," admitted one delegate. Before the convention most knew Ben only by reputation and wondered if he would live up to all the good things said about him—or down to the few bad things. One delegate from Georgia recorded this impression of the "famous Dr. Franklin": "He does not shine much in public council. He is no speaker, nor does he seem to let politics engage his attention. He is, however, a most extraordinary man, and tells a story in a style more engaging than anything I ever heard. . . . He is 82 [sic] and possesses an activity of mind equal to a youth of 25 years of age."

A 1784 MAP OF "THE THIRTEEN UNITED STATES OF AMERICA"

After the Revolutionary War the United States—created from the thirteen British colonies—bordered the east coast of America. But the United States, as this map shows, owned only a small part of the continent. England still controlled Nova Scotia and Newfoundland, in Canada; France owned the territory of Louisiana; and Spain held Florida. Ben, who hoped the United States would one day control all of North America, wrote, "One has merely to look at the map to see America's destiny."

Sense Over Sound

In 1785 officials from the town of Franklin, Massachusetts (named in Ben's honor), asked the seventy-nine-year-old statesman to donate a bell for their town's new meetinghouse. Ben, however, had a better idea:

> I have advised that they spare themselves the expense of a steeple at present, and that they accept books instead of a bell, sense being preferable to sound.

A NEW GOVERNMENT IS BORN

Behind the statehouse doors the delegates drew up a new government. This government would have three branches: a legislative branch that would raise taxes and pass laws; an executive branch led by a president who would carry out the laws and conduct foreign affairs; and a judicial branch, a system of courts that would decide whether or not the government and states acted legally.

It was a good plan, but tempers soon flared as states argued over the issue of representation. The large states demanded that the number of representatives in Congress be based on population, which would give them an advantage over the small states. The small states, fearing they would be overwhelmed by such a system, insisted each state have equal weight in the legislature. Debate over this issue became so heated some delegates threatened to leave. "Does anyone have a way out," cried one, "or should we all go home?" Ben had a way out. He proposed the Great Compromise. It created a House of Representatives, where each state would have one member for every 40,000 inhabitants (later amended to 30,000), and a Senate, in which each state would have an equal number of votes. The delegates agreed to this compromise, and Ben's two-house system of government became the foundation of the Constitution.

The delegates moved on to other issues. What should be the role of the president? Who should be able to vote? Who would print money? And then the thorniest issue— slavery. How should slaves be counted toward representation in the House? Delegates from the states with few slaves did not want to count them at all. They pointed out that since slave owners considered slaves property, those same slaves should not be counted as people. The delegates from the states with many slaves objected. If slaves were not counted as people, they threatened, they would walk away from the convention. The others could not let this

happen. They agreed to count three-fifths of the total number of slaves. They also agreed to ignore the entire slave trade issue until 1808. This compromise made no one happy. But even Ben, who had once owned slaves but had come to detest the institution of slavery, agreed to it. "The Constitution, and thus the United States must be saved from collapse," he said.

On September 8 Gouveneur Morris of Pennsylvania was handed the job of giving the document some literary polish. He added the now famous preamble: "We the people of the United States, in order to form a more perfect union, establish justice, . . . promote the general welfare, and secure the blessings of liberty to ourselves and our posterity, do ordain and establish this Constitution for the United States of America."

By September 17 the Constitution was ready for signing. But some delegates now announced they would not sign. Others remained unsure. With difficulty Ben rose and, because the exertion of standing and speaking was too much for him, asked another delegate to read a speech he had prepared. "In these sentiments, sir, I agree to this Constitution with all its faults if they are such . . . because I doubt . . . whether any other convention may be able to make a better one." His words dispelled most doubts. All but George Mason of Virginia, an unwavering opponent of the slave trade; Edmund Randolph, governor of Virginia; and Elbridge Gerry, the "Grumbletonian," signed the document.

The Constitution did not take effect, however, until nine state legislatures had voted to adopt it. This happened in June 1788, when New Hampshire adopted it, making the Constitution the law of the land. In April 1789 the electoral college unanimously chose George Washington as the country's first president and John Adams as vice president. And so a new government was born.

The Constitution of the United States

What Did You Leave Us?

When Ben left the final session of the Constitutional Convention, a woman stepped into his path. She demanded to know what, after four months of secrecy, he and the other delegates had produced. Ben's reply was typically short, witty, and to the point:
"A republic, if you can keep it."

Death and Taxes

A few months after signing the Constitution, Ben wrote these words to a friend:

Our new Constitution is now established and it has the appearance that promises permanency; but in this world nothing can be said to be certain except death and taxes.

A CHAIR MADE FAMOUS BY BEN'S WORDS

Ben, watching the delegates walk to the front table to sign the Constitution, pointed to a sun carved on the back of a chair. "I have," he said, "often and often, in the course of this session . . . looked at that . . . without knowing whether it was rising or setting: but now at length I have the happiness to know that it is a rising and not a setting sun."

Ben's letter to John Adams, vice president of the United States, petitioning the first Congress to end slavery

In 1787 Ben took on one last cause. He accepted the presidency of the Pennsylvania Society for Promoting the Abolition of Slavery. Using his prestige, as well as his political connections, he lobbied those in power to consider ending slavery, and in February 1790 he petitioned Congress on the subject. Noting Congress had been created to "promote the welfare and secure the blessings of liberty to the People of the United States," he argued that this should be done "without distinction of color," since all people are created by the "same Almighty Being, alike the objects of his care and equally designed for the enjoyment of happiness." To tolerate less, Ben argued, "was to contradict the meaning of the Revolution." Because the petition arrived with Ben's signature, it spurred Congress to debate it. For the next four to six hours, slavery was, for the first time, publicly discussed on the national level. (Though the issue had come up during the Constitutional Convention, those debates were held behind closed doors and under the strictest code of secrecy.) Did Congress have the power to abolish slavery? This was the important question. Representatives from the south claimed Congress could not, because to do so would be to tamper with the property rights of southern states. Both the Constitution and the Bible, they claimed, endorsed slavery. The argument grew so heated that Ben's petition was referred to a committee whose members eventually determined that Congress had no authority to end slavery until 1808, the deadline agreed to

by the signers of the Constitution. After 1808, the committee continued, Congress could do as it wished, as all constitutional restraints would lapse. The committee's decision saddened Ben. He had hoped Congress would take the opportunity to "strike down this ugly blemish." Slavery, he believed, would soon become an issue the nation would be forced to confront.

SLAVES

In 1731, when Ben was twenty-four years old, he wrote this in his newspaper, the *Pennsylvania Gazette*: "The smallpox has now quite left the city. The number of those who died here is exactly 288 . . . 64 of the number were negroes; if these be valued at £30 per head, the loss to the city . . . is near £2,000."

In 1789, when Ben was eighty-three, he wrote these words in an address to the public: "Slavery . . . is an atrocious debasement of human nature. . . . The galling chains that bind his body do also bind his mind and soul."

What happened in those fifty-eight years to change Ben's attitude toward slavery? "I have experienced many instances of being obliged by better information or fuller consideration to change opinions, even on important subjects," he once said.

Ben did own slaves. He bought his first, "a negro man Peter, and his wife, Jemima," when he was forty-two years old. Later he would buy a ten-year-old boy named Othello for his wife, and he accepted a slave named George as partial payment for a debt.

Then in 1757 Ben traveled to England, where slavery was outlawed. Increasingly he found himself trying to defend America against charges of hypocrisy. How, asked the British, could Americans demand liberties and freedoms that they refused to extend to everyone, white or black?

How indeed? Ben wondered. He began to think, really think, about slavery. By the late 1760s he freed his own slaves. And by 1772 he had formed some fierce antislavery opinions. In an article printed in the *London Chronicle* he lashed out against the slave trade. "Can sweetening our tea with sugar be a reason for such cruelty? Can the petty pleasure of taste compensate for so much misery produced among our fellow man . . . by this pestilential, detestable traffic in bodies and souls?"

But Ben still did not see black people as equal until he visited a school for black children in Philadelphia. There he saw firsthand "the natural capacities of the black race." And Ben learned that "their minds are as quick, their memories as strong . . . they are in every respect equal to white children."

In 1787, as president of Pennsylvania, Ben oversaw the passage of laws providing for the gradual elimination of slavery in his state. But freedom wasn't enough. Ben turned his attention to helping freed slaves take their place in society. Children needed schools. Adults needed jobs. As president of the Pennsylvania Abolition Society (formed by the Quakers, a religious group who believed freedom was a gift from God that everyone was entitled to), he wrote a plan whose aim was to restore the black race "to the rightful enjoyment of their civil liberties."

Sadly, Ben did not live to see his hopes fulfilled. "Equal liberty," he wrote just months before his death, "is . . . the birthright of all men."

THOMAS JEFFERSON, ONE OF THE LAST FRIENDS TO VISIT BEN

In March 1790 Thomas Jefferson called on the man who had helped him write the Declaration of Independence. The two spent a quiet afternoon reminiscing. Then Jefferson expressed pleasure upon hearing that Ben was writing his autobiography. "I cannot say much of that," said Ben, "but I will give you a sample of what I shall leave." He handed Jefferson a sheaf of papers, which the younger man promised to read and return. "No," said Ben. "Keep it." Jefferson understood what a marvelous gift he had been given. "The venerable and beloved Franklin," Jefferson later wrote, had left him with a few "handwritten pages of his life."

THE REAL FATHER OF OUR COUNTRY

Ben was the only one of the Founding Fathers (George Washington, John Adams, Thomas Jefferson, James Madison, and Alexander Hamilton, among others) who signed all four of the major documents that made possible America's independence and nationality. These were:

Declaration of Independence, 1776

Treaty of Alliance, 1778

Treaty of Paris, 1783

Constitution of the United States, 1787

A QUESTION OF RELIGION

Although he had been raised in a strict religious household, Ben did not attend worship services or declare himself a member of any organized religion. And for a man who freely gave his opinion on many subjects, he kept his religious thoughts to himself. Just months before his death, however, an old friend wrote to him. "As much as I know of you I have not an idea of your religious sentiments. Would you," he asked, "be so kind as to enlighten an old friend?"

"Here is my creed," Ben replied.

I believe in one God, creator of the universe. That he governs it by his providence. That he ought to be worshipped. That the most acceptable service we render him is doing good to his other children. That the soul of a man is immortal, and will be treated with justice in another life respecting its conduct in this one. . . . As to Jesus of Nazareth . . . I think the system of morals and his religion, as he left them to us, [are] the best the world ever saw or is likely to see, but . . . I have some doubts as to his divinity; though it is a question I . . . have never studied, it is needless to busy myself with it now, when I expect soon an opportunity of knowing the truth with less trouble. . . . I shall only add, respecting myself, that, having experienced the goodness of that Being in conducting me prosperously through a long life, I have no doubt of its continuance in the next, though without the smallest conceit of meriting such goodness.

*Dr. Benjamin Rush,
who took care of Ben during
his final days*

In the last years of his life Ben developed a bladder stone that caused excruciating pain. Bedridden, he took increasing doses of painkillers, which reduced him to skin and bones. Dr. Rush, who constantly attended him, noted that even though Ben was suffering, he remained "for the most part, alert and good-natured." Early in April 1790 Ben developed a respiratory infection. He ran a fever. His breathing grew heavy. He had a painful cough. Still, he managed to rise from his bed and begged Sally to change the sheets so he could "die in a decent manner." Sally told him she hoped he would recover and live many more years. He replied, "I hope not." Later Sally suggested he change his position in the bed in order to breathe easier. "A dying man," he replied, "can do nothing easy."

Busy Ben

How did Ben manage to do so much? No one knows for sure, but perhaps this piece of advice written by Ben and published in *Poor Richard's Almanack*, holds the key:

Early to bed, early to rise, makes a man healthy, wealthy and wise.

BEN'S EPITAPH FOR HIMSELF

Not fearing death, Ben wrote this inscription for his tombstone when he was twenty-two years old—just
for the fun of it. Although the epitaph was not used on Ben's grave, it is a fine summation of the man.

The Body of
B. Franklin,
Printer;
Like the Cover of an old Book,
Its Contents torn out,
And stript of its Lettering and Gilding,
Lies here, Food for Worms.
But the Work shall not be wholly lost:
For it will, as he believ'd, appear once more,
In a new & more perfect Edition,
Corrected and amended
By the Author.

A FOND FAREWELL

As Ben lay on his deathbed in the spring of 1790 he received a letter from his dear friend George Washington. In it Washington included this heartfelt tribute to the elderly statesman who had done so much for his country:

> *If to be venerated for benevolence, if to be admired for talents, if to be esteemed for patriotism, if to be beloved for philanthropy, can gratify the human mind, you have the pleasing consolation to know that you have not lived in vain. . . . Be assured that, so long as I retain my memory, you will be thought of with respect, veneration, and affection by your sincere friend,*
>
> *George Washington*

B. FRANKLIN, L.L.D. F.R.S.

Born at Boston in New England, Jan. 6.th 1706.
Died at Philadelphia, April 17.th 1790.

A BLACK-BORDERED *Massachusetts Magazine* ANNOUNCED BENJAMIN FRANKLIN WAS DEAD

ON APRIL 17, 1790, three months after his eighty-fourth birthday and with his grandsons Temple and Benny at his side, Ben quietly died. As news of his death traveled around the world the many people whose lives he had touched paused in tribute. In Philadelphia twenty thousand people attended his funeral—the largest ever in that city—where he was buried beside his wife, Deborah, in the northwest corner of the Christ Church Cemetery. In the newly formed House of Representatives a motion for official mourning was unanimously passed. And in France the leader of the National Assembly called on his fellow members to wear mourning for three days in homage to the "mighty genius" who had freed men from the fear of both "thunderbolts and tyrants." But it was a personal friend of Ben's, a French scientist named Felix Vicq d'Azyr, who summed up the impact of Ben's death best. "A man is dead," he wrote, "and two worlds are in mourning."

Adieu!

Ben wrote this farewell to a friend:

We are all fellow laborers in the works of mankind. I leave you still in the field, but having finished my day's work, I am going home to bed. Wish me a good night's rest. . . .
Adieu!

BIBLIOGRAPHY

Since the best source on Ben's life is, of course, Ben himself, I used his words and recollections whenever possible in the writing of this book. Although there are many fine published collections of his writings, these are the ones I used:

Franklin, Benjamin. *Autobiography and Other Writings.* Edited by Kenneth Silverman. New York: Penguin Books, 1986.

—*Benjamin Franklin: A Biography in His Own Words.* Edited by Thomas Fleming. New York: Harper and Row, 1972.

—*Benjamin Franklin: His Life As He Wrote It.* Edited by Esmond Wright. Cambridge, Mass.: Harvard University Press, 1990.

—*Benjamin Franklin: Writings.* Edited by J. A. Leo Lemay. New York: Literary Classics of the United States, 1987.

—*The Papers of Benjamin Franklin.* 36 vols, ongoing. Edited by Leonard Labaree et al. New Haven, Conn.: Yale University Press, 1959–2002.

There are also many fine biographies and narrative histories of Ben's life that I used in the creation of this book. They are:

BOYHOOD MEMORIES

Tourtellot, Arthur Bernon. *Benjamin Franklin: The Shaping of Genius: The Boston Years.* New York: Doubleday, 1977.

Van Doren, Carl. *Benjamin Franklin.* New York: Penguin Books, 1991.

Wright, Esmond. *Benjamin Franklin: A Profile.* New York: Hill and Wang, 1970.

THE FAMILY ALBUM

Lopez, Claude-Anne. *The Private Franklin: The Man and His Family.* New York: W. W. Norton, 1975.

Randall, Willard Sterne. *A Little Revenge: Benjamin Franklin and His Son.* Boston: Little, Brown, 1984.

Skemp, Shelia L. *William Franklin: Son of a Patriot, Servant of a King.* New York: Oxford University Press, 1990.

Tagg, James. *Benjamin Franklin Bache and the "Philadelphia Aurora."* Philadelphia: University of Pennsylvania Press, 1991.

THE WRITER'S JOURNAL

Block, Seymour Stanton. *Benjamin Franklin: His Wit, Wisdom, and Women.* New York: Hastings House, 1975.

Granger, Bruce Ingham. *Benjamin Franklin, An American Man of Letters.* Norman, Okla.: University of Oklahoma Press, 1976.

Grover, Eulalie Osgood. *Benjamin Franklin: The Story of Poor Richard.* New York: Dodd, Mead, 1953.

Miller, Clarence William. *Benjamin Franklin's Philadelphia Printing, 1728–1766: A Descriptive Bibliography.* Philadelphia: American Philosophical Society, 1974.

TOKENS OF A WELL-LIVED LIFE

Aldridge, Alfred Owen. *Benjamin Franklin, Philosopher and Man.* Philadelphia: Lippincott, 1965.

Ford, Paul Leicester. *The Many-Sided Franklin.* Freeport, N.Y.: Books for Libraries Press, 1972.

Nolan, J. Bennett. *General Benjamin Franklin: The Military Career of a Philosopher.* Philadelphia: University of Pennsylvania Press, 1936.

Rogers, George L., ed. *Benjamin Franklin's "The Art of Virtue": His Formula for Successful Living*. Eden Prairie, Minn.: Acorn Publishing, 1986.

Wright, Esmond. *Franklin of Philadelphia*. Cambridge, Mass.: Belknap Press of Harvard University Press, 1986.

THE SCIENTIST'S SCRAPBOOK

Cohen, I. Bernard, ed. *Benjamin Franklin's Experiments*. Cambridge, Mass.: Harvard University Press, 1941.

Crowther, J. G. *Famous American Men of Science*. New York: W. W. Norton, 1937.

Fleming, Thomas. *The Man Who Dared the Lightning: A New Look at Benjamin Franklin*. New York: Morrow, 1971.

Lokken, Roy N., ed. *Meet Dr. Franklin*. Philadelphia: Franklin Institute Press, 1981.

REVOLUTIONARY MEMORABILIA

Adams, John. *Papers of John Adams*. Edited by Robert J. Taylor. Cambridge, Mass.: Belknap Press of Harvard University Press, 1979.

Fleming, Thomas. *Liberty: The American Revolution*. New York: Viking, 1997.

Jefferson, Thomas. *The Papers of Thomas Jefferson*. Edited by Julian P. Boyd. Princeton, N.J.: Princeton University Press, 1950.

Lemay, J. A. Leo, ed. *The Oldest Revolutionary: Essays on Benjamin Franklin*. Philadelphia: University of Pennsylvania Press, 1976.

Maier, Pauline. *American Scripture: Making the Declaration of Independence*. New York: Alfred A. Knopf, 1997.

Morgan, David T. *The Devious Dr. Franklin, Colonial Agent: Benjamin Franklin's Years in London*. Macon, Ga.: Mercer University Press, 1996.

SOUVENIRS FROM FRANCE

Dull, Jonathan. *Franklin the Diplomat: The French Mission*. Philadelphia: American Philosophical Society, 1982.

Lopez, Claude-Anne. *Mon Cher Papa: Franklin and the Ladies of Paris*. New Haven, Conn.: Yale University Press, 1966.

Middlekauff, Robert. *Benjamin Franklin and His Enemies*. Berkeley, Calif.: University of California Press, 1996.

Schoenbrun, David. *Triumph in Paris: The Exploits of Benjamin Franklin*. New York: Harper and Row, 1976.

FINAL REMEMBRANCES

Brands, H. W. *The First American*. New York: Doubleday, 2000.

Carr, William George. *The Oldest Delegate: Franklin in the Constitutional Convention*. Newark, N.J.: University of Delaware Press, 1990.

Rush, Benjamin. *The Selected Writings of Benjamin Rush*. Edited by Dagobert D. Runes. New York: Philosophers Library, 1947.

PICTURE SOURCES

The pictorial materials found in this book come from many sources. Some, such as the engravings, woodcuts, and etchings come from centuries-old books, magazines, and newspapers. Others are photographs of original documents, sketches, and items used by Ben, while the portraits and paintings are copies of those found in many art museums and private collections. Most of these materials were created during Ben's lifetime. Some, however, are interpretations of events created at a later date by various artists. Below is a more detailed description of each picture, as well as the individual or institution who made the picture available.

From "Illustrated lessons." Engraving from *Poor Richard Illustrated*, 1859. Courtesy Library of Congress, LCUSZ6211346. frontis

BOYHOOD MEMORIES

View of Boston. From "Collections des Prospects." Engraving by Friedrich Balthasar Leizelt, 177-. Courtesy Library of Congress, LCUSZ6231876. p. 2

The birthplace of Benjamin Franklin. Wood engraving in *Harper's Weekly*, 1872, from pencil sketch by William Wood Thackara done shortly before the house burned down in 1810. Courtesy Library of Congress, LCUSZ61411. p. 3, top

View of Union Street and the Green Dragon Tavern. Wood engraving, c. 1810. Courtesy the Bostonian Society/Old State House. p. 3, bottom

"Cutting the Toe Nails," from *The Art of Swimming*. Woodcut, 1712. Courtesy American Philosophical Society. p. 5, top

"The Whistle." Woodcut from Benjamin Holley's *Life of Benjamin Franklin*, 1890. Courtesy of the Franklin Collection at the Yale University Library. p. 5, bottom

Cotton Mather. Print engraving, 1820. Courtesy Library of Congress, LCUSZ6292308. p. 6, left

The First King's Chapel and the Boston Grammar (Latin) School. Wood engraving, c. 1810. Courtesy the Bostonian Society/Old State House. p. 6, right

Portrayal of a New England school in the 1700s. Lithograph. Courtesy Library of Congress, LCUSZ625809. p. 7

Title page from John Bunyan's *The Pilgrim's Progress*. 1678. Courtesy Rare Books Division, New York Public Library, Astor, Lenox and Tilden Foundation. p. 8, left

Franklin as a printer's apprentice. Wood engraving from *Pictorial Life of Benjamin Franklin*, 1846. Courtesy Library of Congress, LCUSZ6228212. p. 8, right

The *New England Courant*, No. 80, 1723. Facsimile. Courtesy Rare Book Division, Library of Congress, LCUSZ6228244. p. 9

View of Philadelphia. From "Collections des Prospects." Engraving by Friedrich Balthasar Leizelt, 177—. Courtesy of Library of Congress, LCUZ6241171. p. 10, top

Benjamin Franklin as a youth in front of a doorway with a young woman, Deborah Read. Painting by Dill and Collins Company, July 13, 1923. Courtesy Library of Congress, LCUSZ6254174. p. 10, bottom

Sir William Keith. Engraving, 1757. Courtesy New York Public Library, Emmet Collection, Miriam and Ira D. Wallach Division of Art, Prints and Photographs, The New York Public Library, Astor, Lenox and Tilden Foundations. p. 11, left

Interior of an 18th-century printshop. 18th-century engraving. Courtesy Dover Publications. p. 11, right

Franklin and printers supping on hot-water gruel and bread. Woodcut from Benjamin Holley's *Life of Benjamin Franklin*, 1890. Courtesy of the Franklin Collection at Yale University Library. p. 12, top

Benjamin Franklin's departure. Woodcut from Benjamin Holley's *Life of Benjamin Franklin*, 1890. Courtesy of the Franklin Collection at Yale University Library. p. 12, bottom

Benjamin Franklin. Original painting by Robert Feke. Courtesy Harvard University Portrait Collection, bequest of Dr. John Collins Warren, 1856. p. 13

THE FAMILY ALBUM

Benjamin Franklin courts Deborah Read. Woodcut from Benjamin Holley's *Life of Benjamin Franklin,* 1890. Courtesy of the Franklin Collection at Yale University Library. p. 14, top

Deborah Franklin. Original painting by Benjamin Wilson, 1759. Courtesy American Philosophical Society. p. 14, bottom

Franklin at desk. Painted by David Rent Etter, c. 1830. Courtesy of CIGNA Museum and Art Collection. p. 16

William Franklin. Original painting by Mather Brown, 1769. Courtesy Collection of Mrs. Jackson C. Boswell, Frick Art Reference Library. p. 17

Francis Folger Franklin. Engraving by H. B. Hall after the painting by Samuel Johnson, 1865. Courtesy of the Rare Books Division, The New York Public Library, Astor, Lenox and Tilden Foundation. p. 18, top

Sarah Franklin Bache. Engraving from Paul Leicester Ford's *The Many-Sided Franklin,* 1899. Courtesy Library of Congress, LCUSZ629836. p. 18, bottom

High Street. Engraving by William Birch in *The City of Philadelphia,* 1800. Courtesy Library of Congress, LCUSZ623239. p. 19, left

A New England kitchen. Engraving, 1876. Courtesy Library of Congress, LCUSZ621857. p. 19, right

"To Be Let—the Mansion House of the Late Dr. Franklin." Woodcut by Benjamin Franklin Bache, 1790. Courtesy of the Franklin Collection at Yale University Library. p. 19, bottom

William Temple Franklin. Engraving from Paul Leicester Ford's *The Many-Sided Franklin,* 1899. Courtesy Library of Congress, LCUSZ6240424. p. 20, top

Franklin and family at tea in the garden. Illustration by Holly Pribble after a painting by Jean Leon Gerome, 1787. p. 20, bottom

THE WRITER'S JOURNAL

Benjamin Franklin selling his ballads on the streets of Boston. Painting by C. E. Mills, 1914. Courtesy Library of Congress, LCUSZ6248918. p. 22

Printing press used by Benjamin Franklin between 1725 and 1726. Photograph by the Smithsonian Institution. Courtesy Library of Congress, LCUSZ6246688. p. 23, top

Franklin outside the door of his printing shop. Painting by J. Ferris, June 14, 1910. Courtesy Library of Congress, LCUSZ6254187. p. 23, bottom

Pennsylvania Gazette. September 25–October 2, 1729. Courtesy the Library Company of Philadelphia. p. 24

Frontispiece of *Poor Richard's Almanack,* 1743. Courtesy Library of Congress, LCUSZ629541. p. 26

Illustrated lessons. Engraving from *Poor Richard Illustrated,* 1859. Courtesy Library of Congress, LCUSZ6211346. p. 27

Illustrated chart found in *Poor Richard's Almanack.* Woodcut with letterpress by Benjamin Franklin. Courtesy Library of Congress, LCUSZ6249991. p. 28

Title page from the *General Magazine and Historical Chronicle.* January 1741. Courtesy Library of Congress, LCUSZ6258140. p. 29, top

Frontispiece from "The Way to Wealth," broadside by Benjamin Franklin, 1785. Courtesy Rare Books Division, Library of Congress, LCUSZ6228222. p. 29, bottom

Manuscript of "Dialogue Between Dr. Franklin and the Gout," with Madame Brillon's corrections. Original manuscript by Benjamin Franklin, October 1780. Courtesy American Philosophical Society. p. 30

Benjamin Franklin's *Autobiography,* first page. Original manuscript by Benjamin Franklin, 1771. Courtesy Henry E. Huntington Library and Art Gallery. p. 31

Noah Webster. Engraving by J. Rogers after the painting by S. F. B. Morse. Courtesy Library of Congress, LCUSZ6258140. p. 32

Benjamin Franklin, editor and writer. Painting by Charles E. Mills, c. 1909. Courtesy Library of Congress, LCD419169. p. 33

TOKENS OF A WELL-LIVED LIFE

Benjamin Franklin in fur collar. Painting by unknown American artist after a portrait by Joseph Siffred Duplessis, c. 1830. Courtesy CIGNA Museum and Art Gallery. p. 34

Advertising card for the Junto. Illustration by Holly Pribble after a 1731 woodcut. p. 36, top

Franklin opening the first subscription library in Philadelphia. Painting by Charles E. Mills, c. 1914. Courtesy Library of Congress, LCUSZ6245113. p. 36, bottom

An 18th-century lamplighter. Illustration by Holly Pribble. p. 37, left

Benjamin Franklin, the fireman. Painting by Charles Washington Wright, c. 1850. Courtesy CIGNA Museum and Art Collection. p. 37, right

Exterior view of the American Philosophical Society. Photograph from WPA Project Files, 1933. Courtesy Library of Congress, HABSPA-1464. p. 38, top

Pennsylvania Hospital. Lithograph, c. 1810. Courtesy Library of Congress, LCUSZ6256359. p. 38, bottom

University of Pennsylvania. Wood engraving in *American Magazine,* 1836. Courtesy Library of Congress, LCUSZ6250551. p. 39

Franklin money. Photograph by Bonnie Bandurski. Courtesy Bonnie Bandurski. p. 41

Post rider. Woodcut. Date unknown. Courtesy American Antiquarian Society. p. 42

Map of the country on the Ohio and Muskingham. Engraving by Thomas Hutchins, 1765. Courtesy Rare Book Division, Library of Congress, LCUSZC44809. p. 44

Franklin directing the building of a stockade fort. Painting by Charles E. Mills, c. 1900. Courtesy Library of Congress, LCD1428052. p. 45, left

"The March of the Paxton Men." Woodcut by Henry Dawkins, 1764. Courtesy Library Company of Philadelphia. p. 45, right

THE SCIENTIST'S SCRAPBOOK

A Boyhood experiment. Illustration by Holly Pribble after an illustration from *The Works of Benjamin Franklin,* 1852. p. 46

A "magic square of squares." Engraving by J. Hulett in Benjamin Franklin's *Experiments and Observations on Electricity,* plate v, 1774. Courtesy Library of Congress, LCUSZ6228247. p. 47

The Franklin stove. Engravings by Martinet after sketches by Benjamin Franklin, in *Oeuvres de M. Franklin,* vol. II, plate v, 1773. Courtesy Library of Congress, LCUSZ6228244. p. 48

Benjamin Franklin's electrical apparatus, 1751. Engraving in Benjamin Franklin's *Experiments and Observations on Electricity,* plate 1, 1774. Courtesy Rare Books Division, Library of Congress, LCUSZ6228240. p. 49, top

Electrostatic machine invented by Benjamin Franklin. Photograph by Charles F. Penniman Jr. Courtesy of The Historical and Interpretive Collections of The Franklin Institute, Philadelphia, PA. p. 49, bottom

Title page of Benjamin Franklin's *Experiments and Observations on Electricity.* Published in London, 1751. Courtesy Rare Book Division, Library of Congress, LCUSZ6258219. p. 50

Franklin and kite. Painting by unknown American artist after a painting by Benjamin West, c. 1830. Courtesy CIGNA Museum and Art Collection. p. 51

Leyden jar. Painting by Eric Rohmann. p. 52

The lightning rod. Engraving from Benjamin Franklin's *Experiments and Observations on Electricity,* 1751. Courtesy Library of Congress. LCUSZ6228241. p. 53, top

Franklin the electrician. Engraving by Edward Fisher after a 1762 portrait by Mason Chamberlin. Courtesy Library of Congress, LCUSZ621434. p. 53, bottom

Armonica designed by Benjamin Franklin, 1761. Engravings by Martinet in *Oeuvres de M. Franklin*, plate VII, 1773. Courtesy Rare Book Division, Library of Congress, LCUSZ6228248. p. 54, top

Chart showing the course of the Gulf Stream. Engraving based on diagrams by Benjamin Franklin, 1769. Courtesy of the Franklin Collection at Yale University Library. p. 54, bottom

Mastodon bones found in Big Bone Lick, Kentucky. Engraving, 1767. Courtesy American Philosophical Society. p. 55, top

Letter to Polly Stevenson from Benjamin Franklin in phonetic alphabet. Original manuscript by Benjamin Franklin, July 20, 1768. Courtesy American Philosophical Society. p. 55, bottom

Bifocals invented and worn by Benjamin Franklin, 1784. Courtesy The Historical and Interpretive Collections of The Franklin Institute, Philadelphia, PA. p. 56, left

German version of the fresh-air bath. Illustration by Holly Pribble after c. 1768 engraving. p. 56, right

REVOLUTIONARY MEMORABILIA

Benjamin Franklin thumb portrait. Painting by David Rent Etter after the portrait by David Martin, c. 1830. Courtesy CIGNA Museum and Art Collection. p. 59, top left

King George III. Engraving of an original portrait by Sherburne Studio, 1768. Courtesy Library of Congress, LCUSZ6215553. p. 59, bottom

Number 7 Craven Street. Painting by Eric Rohmann after a pencil drawing, 186–. p. 59, right

British stamp used in the colonies under the Stamp Act, 1760s. Courtesy the Connecticut Historical Society. p. 60, left

Burning of the stamps. Engraving by Daniel Berger after Daniel Chodowiecki, 1784. Courtesy Library of Congress, LCUSZ623762. p. 60, right

Franklin's examination before the House of Commons in London, 1766. Reproduction of a painting by Charles E. Mills, c. 1920. Courtesy Library of Congress, LCUSZ6248920. p. 61

"The Repeal ov the Funeral Procession of Miss Americ-Stamp." Etching with engraving, March 18, 1766. Courtesy Library of Congress, LCUSZ621505. p. 62

The Colonies Reduced. Woodcut by Benjamin Franklin, 1766. Courtesy Library of Congress, LCUSZ6228227. p. 63

A society of patriotic ladies at Edenton in North Carolina. Mezzotint by Philip Dawe [?], 1775. Courtesy Library of Congress, LCUSZ6212711. p. 64, top

British officers preparing to embark with soldiers. Photograph of painting by F. C. Yohn, between 1910 and 1930. Courtesy Library of Congress, LCD419184. p. 64, bottom

The bloody massacre, March 5, 1770. Engraving by Paul Revere, 1770. Courtesy Library of Congress, LCUSZC44600. p. 65

Casting tea overboard in Boston Harbor. Engraving in *Harper's Monthly*, vol. IV, 1851. Courtesy Library of Congress, LCUSZ6253777. p. 66

"America in Flames." Woodcut in *Town and Country* magazine, vol. VI, January 1775. Courtesy Library of Congress, LCUSZC45288. p. 67

Benjamin Franklin before the Privy Council, Whitehall Chapel, 1774. Engraving by Whitechurch after the painting by Christian Schussele, 1859. Courtesy Library of Congress, LCUSZ625849. p. 68, top

Lady Howe checkmating Franklin. Painting by F. May, 18—. Courtesy Yale University Art Gallery, Manson Collection. p. 68, bottom

The Battle of Lexington, April 19, 1775. Engraving by Amos Doolittle after Ralph Earle, 1775. Courtesy Library of Congress, LCD4187746. p. 69

Benjamin Franklin's credentials to the Continental Congress, May 6, 1775. Detail from original manuscript. Courtesy the National Archives, Washington, D.C., Loc. A11, 131A, 15/01/5, Box 10. p. 70, left

Exterior of Philadelphia's statehouse. Photograph from WPA Project Files, 1933. Courtesy Library of Congress, LCD412937. p. 70, right

George Washington. Photograph of picture by Charles Willson Peale, 1913. Courtesy of Library of Congress, LCD43T0150260. p. 71

Title page of Thomas Paine's *Common Sense.* Printed in Philadelphia, 1776. Courtesy Library of Congress, LCUSZ6210658. p. 72, left

Committee of Congress drafting the Declaration of Independence. Engraving and etching by T. D. Booth, 1851. Courtesy Library of Congress, LCUSZ6217878. p. 72, right

John Adams. Lithograph after a painting by Gilbert Stuart, 1828. Courtesy Library of Congress, LCUSZ6213002. p. 72, bottom

Thomas Jefferson rough draft of the Declaration of Independence, first page. Original manuscript. Courtesy the National Archives, Washington D.C., 064-Ft-10A. p. 73

Benjamin Franklin signing the Declaration of Independence. Reproduction of a painting by Charles E. Mills, c. 1911. Courtesy Library of Congress, LCUSZ6292309. pp. 74-75

The Declaration of Independence. Original manuscript. Courtesy the National Archives, Washington D.C., 05-6501. p. 76

The first announcement of the Declaration of Independence, July 4, 1776, outside Independence Hall with Hancock, Franklin, Jefferson, Adams, Livingston, and Sherman on the steps. Engraving by Davis Garber, 1874. Courtesy Library of Congress, LCUSZ6255. p. 77, top

"Join, or Die." Metal cut by Benjamin Franklin in the *Pennsylvania Gazette,* May 9, 1754. Courtesy Library of Congress, LCUSZ629701. p. 77, bottom

SOUVENIRS FROM FRANCE

Franklin in fur hat. Original painting by John Trumball, 1780. Courtesy Yale University Art Gallery. p. 78

King Louis XVI. Photomechanical print from painting by A. F. Callet, c. 1900. Courtesy Library of Congress, LCUSZ6296750. p. 79, left

"Coiffure a l'Independence." Painting by Eric Rohmann. p. 79, middle

Franklin surrounded by the ladies of the French court. Illustration by Holly Pribble after painting by Baron Jolly, 182—. p. 79, right

Exterior of the palace at Versailles. Photograph c. 1890–1900. Courtesy Library of Congress, LCDIGppmsc05387. p. 79, bottom

View of Passy. Illustration by Holly Pribble after an aquatint by Madame Brillon, 1779. p. 80, top

"The Plan," or scene in the French cabinet. Etching published September 1779. Courtesy Library of Congress, LCUSZC45282. p. 80, bottom

Benjamin Franklin as ambassador from the Congress of America to the Court of France. Etching after the medal first done by Manufacture Nationale des Sevres, 1778. Courtesy Library of Congress, LCUSZ6245241. p. 81, left

Arthur Lee. Etching by H. B. Hall, 1869. Courtesy Library of Congress, LCUSZ6116. p. 81, right

Profile of his grandfather, Benjamin Franklin, in margin of his notebook. Original sketch by Benjamin Franklin Bache, 1790. Courtesy American Philosophical Society. p. 82, left

Franklin with a young lady on his knees. Original sketch by Charles Willson Peale, 1767. Courtesy American Philosophical Society. p. 82, right

Portrait of Madame Helvétius. Illustration by Holly Pribble after the portrait by Louis-Michel Van Loo. p. 8^3

Political electricity, or an historical and prophetical print in the year 1778. Engraving 1778. Courtesy Library of Congress, LCUSZ62116241. p. 84

Washington's retreat at Long Island. Engraving by Wageman, 1860. Courtesy Library of Congress, LCUSZ6296920. p. 86, top

The signing of the treaty between France and the U.S. Painting by Charles E. Mills, c. 1920. Courtesy Library of Congress, LCUSZ6248919. p. 86, bottom

Benjamin Franklin's first audience in France at Versailles, March 20, 1778. Etching by Daniel Chodowiecki, 1784. Courtesy Library of Congress, LCUSZ6219420. p. 87

"Combat memorable entre le Pearson et Paul Jones." Etching by Balthasar Leizelt after a painting by Richard Paton, between 1779 and 1790. Courtesy Library of Congress, LCUSZ6297628. p. 88

Surrender of Lord Cornwallis at Yorktown, Virginia, October 19, 1781. Lithograph by Currier and Ives, 1876. Courtesy Library of Congress, LCUSZ6219420. p. 89, top

The American peace commission. Original painting by Benjamin West, 1788. Courtesy Winterthur Museum. p. 89, bottom

Abigail Adams. Engraving from an original painting by Gilbert Stuart, 1860 [?]. Courtesy Library of Congress, LCUSZ6210016. p. 90, top

American eagle. Ink drawing on cardboard, 1898. Courtesy Library of Congress, LCUSZ6249331. p. 90, bottom

Treaty of Paris, signatures and seals of the American commission. Detail from original manuscript, 1783. Courtesy the National Archives, Washington, D.C., photo. no. 59-msc-2-v5-2851-1-58. p. 91

Montgolier balloon rising above a large crowd at Versailles. Engraving, 1783. Courtesy Library of Congress, LCUSZ6242858. p. 92, top

Franklin conquering Mesmer. "Le Magnetisme devoile!" 1784. Courtesy the Franklin Collection at Yale University Library. p. 92, bottom

The reception of Benjamin Franklin. Chromolithography, 1882. Courtesy Library of Congress, LCUSZ6214492. p. 93

FINAL REMEMBRANCES

Franklin's return from France. Painting by Charles E. Mills, c. 1920. Courtesy Library of Congress, LCUSZ6248893. p. 94

Benjamin Franklin. Original painting by Charles Willson Peale, 1787. Courtesy Library of Congress, LCUSZ62101098. p. 95

Franklin in the National Convention. Engraving, 1840. Courtesy Library of Congress, LCUSZ61737. p. 96

Bowles's new pocket map of the United States. Hand-colored map by Carington Bowles, 1784. Courtesy Library of Congress, Historic Map Collection. p. 97

Constitution of the United States. Original manuscript, 1787. Courtesy the National Archives, Washington D.C., 05-6503/1. p. 99

The rising sun, or speaker's chair. Photograph by K.I.S. Courtesy Independence National Historical Park. p. 100, top

Letter to vice president John Adams from Benjamin Franklin. Detail from original manuscript, 1790. Courtesy the National Archives, Washington D.C., SENIA-G3. p. 100, bottom

Thomas Jefferson. Lithography by Pendleton after the original painting by Gilbert Stuart, 1828. Courtesy Library of Congress, LCUSZ62117117. p. 102

Dr. Benjamin Rush. Stipple engraving by St. Memin, 1802. Courtesy Library of Congress, LCUSZ6254697. p. 103

Benjamin Franklin's epitaph. Original manuscript, 1728. Courtesy the Beinecke Rare Book and Manuscript Library, Yale University. p. 104

Benjamin Franklin. Engraving ascribed to Hill in *Massachusetts Magazine*, vol. II, 1790. Courtesy Library of Congress, LCUSZ6231139. p. 105

WEB SITES ABOUT BEN

Autobiography of Benjamin Franklin—The story of Ben's life written by Ben himself.
www.earlyamerica.com/lives/franklin/index.html

Benjamin Franklin: A Documentary History—A scholarly and detailed chronology of Ben's life from J. A. Leo Lemay, a renowned Franklin scholar. Here you will learn about the different stages of Ben's life from printer to elder statesman. Each chapter is broken down year by year.
www.english.udel.edu/lemay/franklin

Benjamin Franklin House—Ben spent most of the years between 1757 and 1775 in England. While there he lived in a house on Craven Street. The process of restoring this house is underway. Learn more about the house and the significance of Ben's years in England.
www.rsa.org.uk/projects/project_closeup.asp?id=1001

Ben Franklin's Pennsylvania Gazette 1728–1800—Read editions of Ben's newspaper.
www.accessible.com

The Friends of Franklin, Inc.—This premier Franklin organization is dedicated to fellowship and learning, and to the spirit of Benjamin Franklin.
www.benfranklin2006.org

The Electric Ben Franklin—The best site about Ben, it includes everything from scholarly articles about various aspects of his life, to fun activities which allow site visitors to tour Declaration Hall, play a game of checkers with Ben, or read grandson Temple's diary.
www.ushistory.org/franklin/

The World of Benjamin Franklin—From Philadelphia's way-cool museum, the Franklin Institute, this kid-friendly site includes a QuickTime movie called "Glimpses of the Man," a very useful Franklin family tree, glossary, and pages devoted to all the men Ben was: inventor, printer, philosopher, etc.
www.fi.edu/franklin/

INDEX